Contents

This book employs a simple rating system to help choose which places to visit:

 'top ten'

◆◆◆ do not miss
◆◆ see if you can
◆ worth seeing if you have time

Introduction and Background

INTRODUCTION

The idea of a Disney Theme Park in Europe goes back nearly 20 years, though it was not until 1984 that The Walt Disney Company began to explore the possibilities seriously. The options were wide open. Would English-speaking Britain, whose citizens so eagerly patronise American Theme Parks, naturally play host to Mickey Mouse? Or should the new Theme Park be blessed with that cocktail of sunshine and oranges so successful in California and Florida – by being located in southern Spain, perhaps? Why not target the

Anything can happen when Mickey gets behind the camera

Parades now take place on what were once fields

wealthy Germans? No doubt they could run the show as efficiently as Walt would have wished. Feasibility studies spawned; Team Disney anguished, and then began some hard bargaining. Eventually, the keys to the kingdom fell into French hands. The promised land was a stretch of unprepossessing sugar-beet fields about 20 miles (32km) east of Paris. Not immediately enticing, but the Marne-la-Vallée area had a number of advantages. For one thing, it was available. And there are not that many suitably-sized tracts of affordable land available in Western Europe these days. Secondly, it lay slap in the middle of a cat's cradle of important communication networks linking the richest and most densely populated countries of Europe. And thirdly, it was on the eastern outskirts of the greater Paris area. It was, admittedly, a bit damper and chillier than one

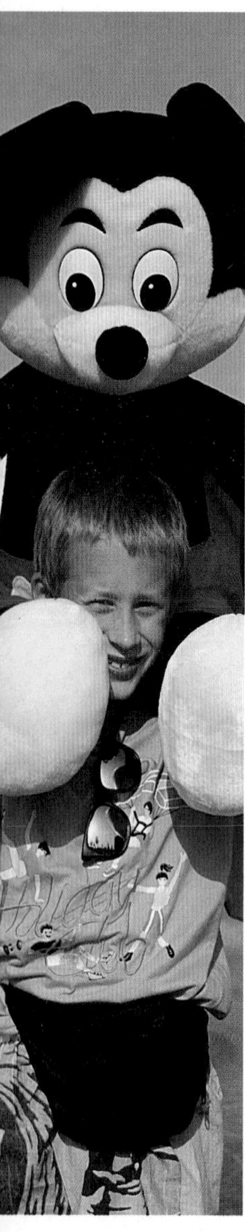

Mickey abounds

might have hoped, but you can't have everything.

The Walt Disney Company signed a 30-year contract to develop the site with the French authorities in 1987. The French government purchased some 4,800 acres (1,940ha) of land, a total area about one-fifth the size of Paris, agreeing to release it to Disney as it was needed. Meanwhile, residents and farmers, now tenants instead of landlords, carried on their lives as normally as they could in a region destined for rapid and irrevocable change. Earth-moving and construction equipment arrived to shift millions of tons of topsoil into new configurations of lakes, railway tracks, road systems and protective circular ramparts, like some Iron Age hill-fort. The statistics were awesome, and the speed at which the project took shape was astonishing. Within four years Phase I of the development had been completed, covering 1,483 acres (600ha) of land. The region was transformed, with 450,000 trees and shrubs, several artificial expanses of water, and almost 20 miles (32km) of roads. Six extraordinary hotels and a 'trapper village' emerged from the fields, but more curious structures could be glimpsed behind the stockade surrounding the new Theme Park – a storybook castle, a piece of recreated Arizona, and a skull-like cave. Meanwhile, around the edges of the complex, speculation buzzed, both of the cerebral and mercenary kinds. Rumours of Disney's sinister transatlantic masterplan to undermine French Culture As We Know It Today were fuelled, and many a pundit had a scornful crack at Mickey Mouse. Not everyone liked the idea of a Theme Park on their doorstep. And, of course, some of the locals had to play the role of dispossessed serfs carefully, to maximise any potential return on their lost land. A crocodile tear or two would not be inappropriate in the circumstances. This controversial climate did not stop entrepreneurs from constructing motels and petrol stations in many of the surrounding villages. These extraneous developments, simply cashing in on the Disney bandwagon, have done most to disrupt the area. Sadly, they

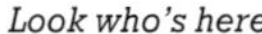

Look who's here

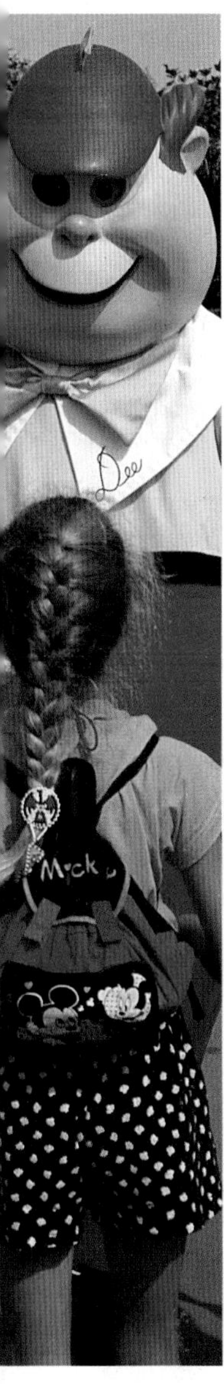

are an inevitable consequence of such a huge investment, readily predictable from all the experiences of American Theme Parks.

Other unintentional effects of Disney's impact on this part of France are less tangible, but still worrying. A glance at local tourist literature produces the disconcerting sensation that the whole of the Seine-et-Marne region is turning into a sort of giant Theme Park. Many local authorities, spurred to commercial enterprise by Disney's example, are now promoting their tourist portfolios strongly as rival (or rather, supplementary) attractions. Every little sight and mildly pretty village is now paraded before the eyes of Disney patrons like some contestant in a game show. Summer pageants, medieval banquets and candlelit tours abound. With all this going on, there is a strong possibility that some visitors at least, dazed by the razzmatazz, will come to regard the great châteaux of the Île-de-France as mere clones of Sleeping Beauty Castle.

For those who recognise the difference, however, the historic and cultural riches of the surroundings (including Paris, of course) must be regarded as one of Disneyland® Resort Paris's most appealing features. In the US, at Orlando and Anaheim, there are certainly dozens of things to do, but they are an oddly monochromatic mix of Theme Parks and contrived recreation. In France the texture of the holiday tapestry is infinitely more interesting and complex.

Controversy has now died down as the positive influence of the Disney Theme Parks on the area's economy is hard to deny. The creation of over 10,000 new jobs and 30,000 in the Île-de-France region, as well as spin-offs for hoteliers and other local businesses, has been most welcome. The infrastructure of the area (road and rail connections, hotel accommodation, and so on) has been boosted out of all recognition. The region and Disney's fans worldwide are ready to welcome the new Walt Disney Studios® Park, which opened its gates a few days before the tenth anniversary of Disneyland® Paris. Then, when the contract expires in the year 2017, *'On verra'*.

The scale and scope of Disneyland® Resort

Paris is by any standards a modern miracle, second in Europe only to the Channel Tunnel in terms of cost and engineering resources. The Sun King himself, Louis XIV, would have appreciated such an ambitious project. But any organisation as powerful as The Walt Disney Company is bound to arouse a certain amount of jealousy and malice; yet, after a disappointing start and some inevitable adjustments, Disneyland® Resort Paris is now firmly taking root in French soil.

Some agonise, justifiably enough, over the unFrenchness of it all. There are nods and winks at European fairy stories and children's classics, but basically Disneyland® Resort Paris is a heartily transatlantic product, as American as a prime rib steak. French culture, however, is nothing if not robust. The

things many people love about France and the French way of life will survive the arrival of Mickey Mouse perfectly well. In any case, before we complain too loudly about the invasion of an alien culture, maybe there are some things about the land of Mickey Mouse that we Europeans should take note of: what, after all, is wrong with clean loos, courteous staff, efficient transport systems and litter-free grounds? For the resort to be a success, all Disney needed was for enough people to turn up and enjoy themselves, and then tell their friends. This goal was easily reached, for enjoying yourself at Disneyland® Resort Paris is almost unavoidable. Where else can grown-up people ride on an elephant roundabout, or wear mouse ears, without feeling like idiots?

Disneyland® Park, from the air

Walt Disney, (1901-66)

BACKGROUND

Walt Disney

Few film producers have captured the imagination, influenced so many people, and aroused such loyalty, loathing and passionate interest as Walt Disney. More than 30 years after his death, debate still rages over the influence of his work – even more over the colossal empire he created to perpetuate it. Through this he has achieved a strangely alarming immortality. So, too, has his single most memorable creation: Mickey Mouse, now over 70 years old.

Walter Elias Disney was born in Chicago, Illinois, in 1901, the fourth of five children in a family of slender means. His father was a struggling building contractor whose varied enterprises consistently failed. When they did, the family doggedly moved on, first to Marceline, then to Kansas City, Missouri. Walt's unsettled upbringing gave him only a rudimentary education, and he spent his spare time living on his wits, delivering newspapers door-to-door and hawking sodas on trains. During a brief stint of ambulance-driving in France at the end of World War I (he was too young to join up), he first exercised his artistic talents commercially, painting camouflage helmets and adding fake bullet holes. After the war Walt returned to Kansas City and found a job drawing for an advertising agency. There he met a talented Dutch artist, Ub Iwerks, and together they set up a company, Laugh-o-Gram Films. It soon went to the wall but, like all true romantics of his day, Walt was hopelessly hooked on the glamour of celluloid. With a small fistful of dollars, he set off to try his luck in Hollywood, followed by Ub. From then on Walt had little contact with his parents. But he always kept up with his elder brother Roy, with whom he later set up in business to produce short cartoons. In 1925 Walt married Lillian Bounds, who lived with his erratic genius for over 40 years.

After many false starts and financial failures (one of which involved the loss of his prize cartoon character, Oswald the Lucky Rabbit, to an unprincipled distributor), Walt's big break

Fantasyland's awe-inspiring castle

came in 1928, using a new character called Mickey Mouse. The film was *Steamboat Willie,* the first animated film to use synchronised sound. Mickey's squeaks and sighs were Walt Disney's own. Roy Disney attempted to temper Walt's wilder impulses with sensible financial caution, but Walt, always cavalier about the money side, was an incorrigible enthusiast, an ideas man, a risk-taker. And his instincts were sound. He could spot a good story at a thousand paces (and shamelessly borrow it, if necessary) and then would edit it brilliantly for his own medium. Above all else, he was a maniacal perfectionist. Every last detail had to be right. All his life he worked obsessively hard, even coming dangerously close to a nervous breakdown in 1931. Slowly the Disney studios began to prosper with full-length animations like *Snow White and the Seven Dwarfs, Pinocchio* and *Fantasia*. After World War II the Disney brothers seized the opportunities offered by the new era of television. Their *Disneyland*® programme (set up, in part, to fund the first Theme Park) was a great success. From animated films, Disney moved on to using live actors in comedies, wildlife pictures and adventure stories like *Treasure Island*. The core of the business was always safe, clean, family entertainment for the post-war era. The films sold like hot cakes.

Today's Disney Theme Parks know no bounds

lly Brown *riverboat*

The Disney Movies
1923 '***Alice Comedies***' (with Ub Iwerks): 56 films mixing animation and live action.
1928 ***Steamboat Willie***: first appearance of Mickey and Minnie Mouse, and the first animated film using synchronised sound. Only squeaks, sighs and whistles were recorded.
1929 '***Silly Symphonies***': 75 short animations in which plants and creatures come to life. The famous Skeleton Dance was the first of this series.
1930 ***The Chain Gang***: first appearance of Pluto.
1932 ***Flowers and Trees***: wins Disney's first Academy Award, and the first cartoon made in *full* colour. *Mickey's Revue* appears – also the first appearance of Goofy.
1934 ***The Wise Little Hen***: Donald Duck first appears.
1935 ***Music Land***.
1937 ***Snow White and the Seven Dwarfs***: the first full-length feature animation. Despite Roy Disney's gloomy predictions and the massive costs, a huge success.
1940 ***Pinocchio*** and ***Fantasia*** appear, denting the studio's budgets, but not its spirit.
1941 ***Dumbo*** wins an Academy Award for Best Original Score.
1942 ***Bambi*** is premiered.
1943 ***Der Führer's Face***: Donald Duck does his bit for the war effort, and the film wins an Academy Award. *Saludos Amigos* appears.
1950 ***Treasure Island*** and ***Cinderella***: *Treasure Island* was a departure from Disney norms, using live actors.
1951 ***Alice in Wonderland***.
1953 ***Peter Pan***, ***The Living Desert*** and ***The Alaskan Eskimo***.
1954 ***20,000 Leagues Under the Sea***: Academy Award for special effects.
1955 ***Davy Crockett – King of the Wild Frontier*** and ***Lady and the Tramp***.
1959 ***Sleeping Beauty***.
1960 ***Swiss Family Robinson***.
1961 ***One Hundred and One Dalmatians***.
1964 ***Mary Poppins***: six Academy Awards, including a Best Actress award for Julie Andrews.
1967 ***The Jungle Book***.

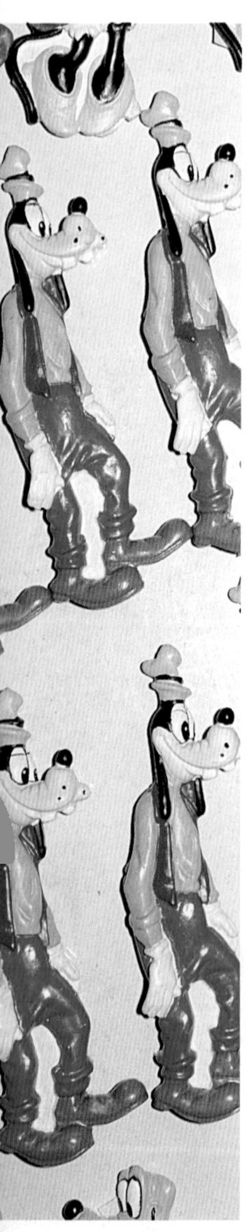

Disney merchandise

1970 ***The Aristocats***
1973 ***Robin Hood***
1977 ***The Many Adventures of Winnie the Pooh***
1988 ***Who Framed Roger Rabbit***: four Academy Awards, signalling Disney's return to success after many uncertain years following Walt's death.
1990 ***The Little Mermaid***: two Academy Awards for musical content.
1991 ***Beauty and the Beast***: two Academy Awards, and nomination as Best Picture.
1993 ***Aladdin***
1994 ***The Lion King***: the biggest box office success ever.
1995 ***Pocahontas***
1996 ***The Hunchback of Notre-Dame***
1998 ***Mulan***
1999 ***Tarzan***
2000 ***Dinosaur***
2001 ***Atlantis***

Magic Kingdoms

Walt first dreamt of Theme Parks in the 1930s, imagining how he could improve on the dreary ones he took his daughters to see, but it was only after the war that his obsession developed to fever pitch. At that time amusement parks were bracketed with funfairs and circuses as tawdry and disreputable places. Walt found it very difficult to convey his vision of a place of fun and fantasy in an orderly, civilised setting. He wanted to create a place where both adults and children could enjoy themselves together and come away feeling better. He wanted themes that reflected his Utopian faith in technological progress and the future, a haven in which the archetypal American virtues of pluck and innocence could flourish.

In 1955 Disneyland® Park (also known as 'the Magic Kingdom'), the world's first Theme Park, opened at Anaheim, in Orange County, California. Roy refused to let Walt have the money to build it; he had to cash in his life insurance. But the enterprise succeeded, and the world flocked to see it. Walt began to dream of other Theme Parks, his ambitions growing like beanstalks for a brave new world – a model of planning and innovative lifestyles. A second site was chosen: the ill-drained acres of central Florida, another 'Orange County'. Quietly the land was purchased on Disney's behalf at knock-down prices through various agencies. Sadly, Walt Disney never lived to see his Floridian dream realised. In 1966 his permanent smoker's cough developed a more sinister note, and by December, just a week after his 65th birthday, he was dead. It was left to his heirs to

Autopia's superhighway of the future

Disney characters are central to all the Park's attractions

construct Walt Disney World Resort from the blueprint. This second Theme Park complex opened in Orlando in 1971, much larger and more ambitious than anything in California. Twelve years later, in 1983, another Disneyland® Park appeared in Tokyo. Soon afterwards, a talented new chief executive recruited from Paramount, Michael Eisner, was setting a firm course for the floundering Disney empire, which for several years after its founder's death had seemed to lose its way. Throughout the 1980s the Theme Parks boomed, and revenues from television and merchandising soared. By the middle of the decade plans for a European park were firmly on the drawing board.

The Disney Ethos

Disney values are decent and clean-living. In his many films, and in the Theme Parks, Walt Disney's touching optimism and trust in the goodness of humanity reign supreme (odd in a man who, by all accounts, trusted no one in business). Disney Theme Parks are worlds of happy endings and moral certainties. They are simplistic stuff by the cynical standards of

Norman Blood?
By a happy and much-publicised coincidence, Walt Disney's ancestry was French. The name 'Disney' is alleged to come from the Normandy coastal village of Isigny-sur-Mer. After the Norman Conquest of England in 1066, Hughes d'Isigny and his son Robert settled there. Gradually the name became abbreviated and Anglicised. One branch of the family is still in Lincolnshire, having kept the more Gallic spelling D'Isney. But Walt's forebears emigrated to Ireland in the 17th century, and from there Arundel Elias Disney and his brother Robert set sail for North America in 1834. Walt's father was actually born in Canada; his mother came from Ohio. It is a tenuous link, but there is at least some justification for the company's claim that France is the natural home of any European version of a Disneyland® Theme Park.

the early 21st century – but they are still popular and, on the surface, seem harmless enough, even charmingly naïve. In Michael Eisner, Disney's current chieftain, the company seems to have found Walt's true successor, someone with the same unerring instinct for mass-market taste. Intellectuals have levelled criticism at the anodyne, sanitised qualities of the Disney message, typically declaring it a 'sickening blend of cheap formulas packaged to sell', and a symptom of a kind of infantilism at the heart of the American psyche.

Imagineers
Any operation on the scale of a Disney Theme Park requires colossal planning and co-operative effort, but just how much goes on behind the scenes may surprise you. A whole workforce of Disney employees called 'Imagineers' devotes its time and energy to inventing and realising the attractions. These artists and technicians are the ones who make illusion reality, working with models and micro-cameras, experimenting with innumerable materials, designs and ideas,

studying every last detail for authenticity. It is a serious business: careers have been made and broken over the height of some of the buildings. The complexity of all this is fascinating, though most of the illusions are hidden or barely perceived by the vast majority of visitors. When you enter Disneyland® Park, notice how far away the castle seems as you look down Main Street. Why do some of the other buildings seem so accessible? It is all done with clever angles and techniques called 'forced perspective'. Upper storeys are often rather smaller than their proper size, with every architectural detail carefully scaled down. These illusions are just 3-D versions of the kinds of things Disney constantly practised in his films. What the eye sees is not necessarily what is really there, as any animation specialist knows.

Audio–Animatronics®

This Disney-patented system of animating figures (animals, plants, birds and robots as well as humans) has now reached levels of great technical sophistication, and some amazingly lifelike effects can be created. Among striking examples of this new technology are the rowdy pirates in Adventureland, and the robots of Discoveryland. Best of all, without a doubt, is the wonderful dragon that lurks beneath the castle.

Cast Members

Anywhere else, these people would be called Theme Park staff. But here they are the cast – everyone from that fellow patiently sweeping up spilt popcorn to Sleeping Beauty herself. The whole park is a theatrical performance. How do they rehearse for that relentless PR exercise, constantly smiling and helpful? They go to university! The Disney University, where appropriate cheerful responses are drilled into prospective members, and deviant tendencies like tattoos, red nail polish and facial hair are rigorously drilled out. However, some concessions have been made to French fashion: red lipstick may be worn, tastefully. And who are you? Never mere 'customers' – you are the *guests* at this show.

THEME PARK TIPS

It is well worth spending some time familiarising yourself with the layout of Disneyland® Resort Paris and the Theme Parks, particularly if you only have one or two days to see everything. Those hours spent in the Parks will be expensive if you waste time, but if you use them well you will not be disappointed. Look at the maps of the Theme Parks, or better still inside the seasonal Disneyland® Resort Paris Official Holiday Guide (brochures). Although not to scale, they both show Disney® Village, the parking area and hotels, including Disney's Davy Crockett Ranch®, in relation to the Theme Parks.

The striking, pink and turreted Disneyland® Hotel

Disneyland® Resort Paris

Disneyland® Resort Paris covers a total land area of about 1,500 acres (600ha). When you hear that there is still room for development, you realise the gigantic proportions of the whole project! At present the resort includes seven themed hotels, including a trapper village with campsite, a 27-hole golf course, the Disney® Village entertainment centre, the Disneyland® Park, which alone represents 140 acres (57ha), and the new Walt Disney Studios® Park, 62 acres (25ha) at opening stage.

Exit roads from surrounding routes lead smoothly along newly constructed dual carriageways to all parts of the Resort, with all hotels and the main car park clearly sign-posted from exit 14 of the A4 motorway. If you are heading for the campsite, which is situated at **Disney's Davy Crockett Ranch®**, however, you should take exit 13 from the A4. If you need petrol, you will find it by **Disney's Hotel Santa Fe®**. From the large visitor's car park (remember in which section you leave your vehicle), covered moving walkways lead to a wide avenue that heads straight for the parks' entrance and ticket offices past the film-set decor of Disney® Village on the left. The entrance gates of the Walt Disney Studios® Park are opposite the glass dome of the RER station. Further on, beside the unmissable **Disneyland® Hotel** is the entrance to the Disneyland® Theme Park. If you have a pet, you must leave it at the **Animal Care Center** next to the parking area, where a service charge applies (see Charges, page 26).

At the end of the moving walkways there is a picnic area. There is a car park for disabled visitors nearer the entrance. If you arrive by commuter train you will emerge at the Marne-la-Vallée–Chessy RER station, very close to the entrance to both Parks. There is a post office inside the station. Next to it is the TGV-Eurostar station, terminal point of the express link joining all European rail networks. Several expanses of artificially created water form scenic vistas within the resort area. **Lake Disney®** is surrounded by three hotels, each representing a typical aspect of the American scene: **Disney's Hotel New York®**, **Disney's Sequoia Lodge®** and **Disney's Newport Bay Club®**. Two more hotels, **Disney's Hotel Santa Fe®** and **Disney's Hotel Cheyenne®**, straddle the Rio Grande, a canal northeast of Lake Disney®. There are traffic-free promenades on either side of the water, making the route between the Theme Parks and the Resort Hotels a pleasant walk, but a free shuttle bus is available. **Disney's Davy Crockett Ranch®**, situated at the heart of a forested area and symbolising the American pioneer spirit, it is a 15-minute drive to the Theme Parks.

Disneyland® Park in Figures

- Over 100 million visitors in nine years
- 10,500 Cast Members of 50 different nationalities
- 43 attractions, 80 per cent of which are covered
- 700 actors and dancers, 50 musicians, 150 designers, artists and decorators, 100 technicians, 30 dressmakers and 14 hours of live entertainment programmed daily
- More than one million light bulbs used for the Main Street Electrical Parade
- Up to 150,000 meals served daily during peak periods
- 26 million items sold every year in 42 shops and 23 stands

The entrance to Disney® Village

Disney® Village
Opposite the RER station is an eye-catching complex that looks like a film set, or rather several contrasting film sets, recreating the atmosphere of typical American towns: angular metallic structures linked by a cat's cradle of wires tower above ochre-coloured saloons and bars along a wide avenue extending to the edge of Lake Disney®, beyond the huge globe of the deliberately flashy Planet Hollywood restaurant. During the day the sun glitters on the shiny aluminium and mosaic panels; at night the area is a maze of starry lights rocking to the sound of live concerts all year round. This bold modern structure was designed by Californian architect Frank Gehry and is Disneyland® Resort Paris's principal entertainment centre apart from the Theme Parks. It aims to offer alternative entertainment, eating and shopping facilities to Theme Park visitors during the day and keep them happy after the Parks' gates have closed. It consists of shops, restaurants, bars and various night spots, including a nightclub and the popular **Buffalo Bill's Wild West Dinner Show**, as well as 15 cinemas (with a total seating capacity of 3,658; English films are also shown). Practical facilities include the tourist information bureau for the Île de France region, an American Express office and a parking area. The Disney® Village complex is open every day and there is no entrance charge except on 31 December.

Theme Parks
A practical approach is necessary if you wish to make the most of a day of non-stop entertainment in the magic world of Disney. Both Theme Parks provide useful services to make sure that you enjoy yourself to the full. Bulky articles you will not need during your visit can be handed in at **Guest storage** (service charge), situated outside the Disneyland® Park entrance, close to the Guest Relations office, and just inside Walt Disney Studios® Park, next to Studios Services. Once through the gates, you are ready to begin your journey and will want to get your bearings as quickly as possible; look at the map given to you on arrival: Walt Disney Studios® Park is divided into four distinct production areas starting with the Front Lot, overlooked by the tall water tower. Disneyland® Park is also divided, rather like a pie chart, into five separate thematic areas or lands: beyond Main Street, U.S.A. stretching ahead of you, lies the park's central landmark, Sleeping Beauty Castle, its spindly turrets thrusting into the Île-de-France sky. But once inside the Parks, do not be dazzled by the lure of the 108-feet (33-metre)-high Studios Water Tower, or the enchanting Sleeping Beauty Castle. Instead take time to look around Walt Disney Studios® Park's Mediterranean courtyard or Disneyland® Park's turn-of-the-century main square, because here is where you will find some extremely useful facilities and services.

Studio Services (Walt Disney Studios® Park) and **City Hall** (Disneyland® Park), both situated just inside the gates, are the parks' main information centres and are well worth a visit: they are a convenient meeting place for families and friends, and messages can also be left for them. Guide maps in several languages, Park information, Entertainment programmes, Disabled Guest Guides and information in Braille are available at the desks, where you can also book a room, a restaurant, a dinner-show or a Character Tea; check the times of the shows and parades on offer in the Parks; change your money at the American Express Foreign Currency Exchange; or make reservations for a guided walking tour of either or both parks (one-hour tours of Walt Disney Studios® Park, two-hour tours of Disneyland® Park).

The traditional American Market House Deli in Main Street, U.S.A.

If it's a **pushchair** or **wheelchair** you need, then you can hire one by the day near Studio Services in Walt Disney Studios® Park or across Town Square from City Hall in Disneyland® Park; a padlock is useful to keep your pushchair safe while you take young children on rides. Note that Cast Members are not available to accompany guests in wheelchairs or to look after children while their parents enjoy attractions that are unsuitable for young children. However, Disneyland® Resort

Paris has found a way to alleviate adult frustration in this case: it's called '**baby switch**' and it allows parents to do the attraction without having to stand in the queue twice (information from the Cast Members at the entrance to the attraction).
The **Lost and Found office** is next to Studio Services at the entrance to Walt Disney Studios® Park and at City Hall in Disneyland® Park.
Before you leave the Town Square to explore the rest of Disneyland® Park, bear in mind that it is a good place to watch the Parade and take pictures from different angles as the floats slowly make their way round the square; a spot is reserved for people in wheelchairs in front of Ribbons & Bows Hat Shop.
Now that you have everything you need and are in the right mood to make the most of your visit, you can uncover the magic

The Disneyland® Park entrance is always a scene of bustling activity

of cinema at Walt Disney Studios® Park. Or at Disneyland® Park, you can walk down Main Street, U.S.A., hop on one of the nostalgic vehicles bound for **Central Plaza** or embark on a journey round Disneyland® Park aboard one of the steam trains of the **Disneyland® Railroad**. When you get to Central Plaza, you will see the Plaza Gardens Restaurant on your right; next to it are three more services that might prove useful at some time during your visit: the **First Aid Center**, the **Baby Care Center** and the **Lost Children Office**. All three are also located behind Studio Services in Walt Disney Studios® Park.

Should you need to draw cash while you are inside one of the theme parks, you will find **automatic cash dispensers** next to Studio Services and at Backlot Express Restaurant in Walt Disney Studios® Park, as well as in the arcades parallel to Main Street, U.S.A., in Adventureland and in Discoveryland inside Disneyland® Park.

Some Don'ts

- Smoking, eating and drinking are not allowed inside attractions and in queuing areas. Restaurants are divided into smoking and non-smoking sections. A picnic area located between Guest Parking and the Theme Parks Entrance is intended for guests bringing their own food.
- No pets, except guide dogs, are allowed to enter the parks. They may be left at the Animal Care Center near the car park on production of a certificate of health, or verification of vaccination. A service charge applies (see Charges, page 26).
- Do not leave personal belongings unattended.
- No flash photography or video taping are allowed inside the attractions.

General Guidelines

In this book, which went to press before the opening of Walt Disney Studios® Park, attractions in Disneyland® Park

Intergalactic enthusiasts adore Star Tours in Discoveryland

And Some Dos

- Remember to bring a sweater, light rainwear and to wear comfortable shoes.
- Shoes and shirts must be worn at all times.
- Reduce waiting time by making use of the Fastpass service (see page 30)
- Children under seven must be accompanied by an adult.
- Get a hand-stamp if you leave either Theme Park so that you can get back in again later, and make sure you have your Park Ticket(s) with you.
- Check on closing times.
- Pick up an **Entertainment Program** from City Hall in Disneyland® Park or from Studio Services in Walt Disney Studios® Park.
- Life is easier if you use a credit card. Visa, Mastercard or American Express are widely accepted. Guests staying at a Disneyland® Resort Paris hotel you will be given a chargecard that can be used within the Theme Parks.
- Visit the tourist office next to the RER station if you are thinking about touring outside the Theme Park (tel: 01 60 43 33 33, daily 9am–10pm).

alone are given ratings – from one to three stars. A tick used in conjunction with the star ratings indicates an attraction that is considered to be one of the 'top ten' in the park (see also page 3). Every ride is someone's favourite, and someone else's least favourite. You will not know if you like something unless you try it, so try not to prejudge anything. Have a go!

Opening times, operating procedures and so on are subject to change without notice, and it is always advisable to check with Guest Relations for up to date information.

Disney Theme Parks Entrance Tickets

There are two tiers of charges: one for children aged between

Charges
These prices are intended as a guide, and were current at the time of going to press. Prices should be checked with Disneyland® Resort Paris at the time of your visit.
1-day Theme Park Entrance Ticket (high or low-season): Adults €36, €27, Children (3-11) €29, €23
3-day 'Hopper' Ticket: Adults €99, €73, Children €80, €62
2-Park Annual Ticket: Adults €229, Children, €199
Car parking: €7 per day
Shuttle Buses Airport buses: €12.96 (single adult fare); €9.91 (child fare)
RER from central Paris: €5.95 (single adult fare); €2.95 (child)
Animal Care Center: €8 per day (including food), or €12 overnight
Wheelchair or pushchair rental: €6.10 per day (not to be taken outside the Theme Parks)
Buffalo Bill's Wild West Show (Disney Village): Adults €49.50; Children €29.50 (drinks and dinner included).
Hotels: Prices vary according to season and category of hotel; in summer, two nights (based on two adults and two children sharing a room), including continental breakfast and unlimited access to both Disney Theme Parks for three days, ranges from around €170 to €312 per adult and €82 per child.
Disney's Davy Crockett Ranch®: The same formula (based on three adults and three children sharing a cabin) costs around €167 per adult and €80 per child.

three and eleven inclusive and one for anyone aged twelve or over. Children under three enter free of charge. In addition, you can buy an Entrance Ticket for one or three days (the extended ticket is cheaper pro rata than the one-day ticket); it does not have to be used on consecutive days but must be used within the three-year validity period. Annual Entrance Tickets are also available, giving unlimited entry for one year. Entrance charges are subject to constant revision (not necessarily upwards, either – Disney is well aware of market forces). Your Entrance Ticket entitles you to

Keep your Entrance Ticket handy

Honey, I Shrunk the Audience, at Disneyland® Park

unlimited use of any of the attractions, shows and parades within the Theme Park of your choice (one-day ticket) or both Theme Parks (three-day ticket) during operating hours, except the Rustler Roundup Shootin' Gallery in Frontierland and the Video Games Arcade in Discoveryland in the Disneyland® Park (€2 a go – 2002 price).
Occasionally attractions may be closed for technical reasons (such as safety checks).

Opening Times
For full details, see the **Directory** section on page 118.

Planning Your Visit

Your action plan depends very much on what sort of ticket you have. If you have bought just a one-day Entrance Ticket, you will first have to decide which theme park you want to visit. If you choose Walt Disney Studios® Park, your ticket also entitles you to enter Disneyland® Park three hours before closing time. If you prefer to spend the day in Disneyland® Park, you will have to tackle the Theme Park like a military exercise if you want to see it all. Get there early and head for the popular rides first (**Big Thunder Mountain** or **Space Mountain**), making the most of slack periods (for example, during mealtimes or in the evening). You will obviously get more value out of your ticket if you choose a time when Disneyland® Park stays open late (in summer, or at peak holiday times). A useful time-saver is

Disney® Village comes alive when the Theme Parks closes

the free Fastpass service available at five attractions in Disneyland® Park and at three attractions in Walt Disney Studios® Park (see page 30). With a three day Entrance Ticket, you have more time to experience the two Theme Parks. In addition, you can take a rest whenever you like, and do the things you like best more than once. If you are staying at Disneyland® Resort Paris for several days, it is a good idea to have a break from the Theme Parks at some point to get in touch with reality again – tour an area of France, or go to Paris. Then come back and have another day. Most people can have a good two days' fun out of Disneyland® Park; keen theme-parkers like to stay even longer. What if you hate it once you get inside? Well, it is true that not everyone likes Theme Parks. The chances are, though, that you will want more time than you actually have available. If you do buy a three-day ticket, do not try to see the whole of either Theme Park on day one. Save some of the excitement for your next visit. In Disneyland® Park visit Main Street U.S.A., the castle, Fantasyland and Discoveryland on day one, and then go to Frontierland and Adventureland on day two. You can try out your favourite rides

Quick Visits
If you have only one day, or just want a rapid tour of Disneyland® Park, these are the things you should definitely catch (but see **Contra-indications** on page 31).
Sleeping Beauty Castle
Big Thunder Mountain
Honey, I Shrunk the Audience
Phantom Manor
Pirates of the Caribbean
Space Mountain
Star Tours
Main Street Electrical Parade
Fantasy in the Sky
Fireworks (seasonal only).

Fastpass
This free service is designed to cut waiting times at the following popular attractions.
In Disneyland® Park: Indiana Jones™ and the Temple of Peril: Backwards!, Space Mountain – from the Earth to the Moon, Big Thunder Mountain, Peter Pan's Flight, Star Tours
In Walt Disney Studios® Park: Studio Tram Tour featuring Catastrophe Canyon, Rock'n' Roller Coaster starring Aerosmith, Flying Carpets Over Agrabah
By inserting your Park Ticket into the distributor machine at the attraction of your choice, you will receive a ticket for a one hour time slot. If you return to the attraction during this time, you should be able to enter within a short time, thus avoiding the traditional waiting time.
Note that this service is subject to availability and it is advisable to visit popular attractions as early possible

again, have a relaxing lunch, look round all the shops, or even leave the Theme Park for a nap or a swim at your hotel on day three. Here is a brief run-down of attractions, showing which ones are best for which people, (see also **Children,** page 104).

Young Children
Very young children will best enjoy the rides on **Main Street, U.S.A**, the **Sleeping Beauty Castle** and **Fantasyland** with its fairytale theme rides: **Peter Pan**, **Les Voyages de Pinocchio** (Pinocchio's Travels), or **Blanche-Neige et les Sept Nains** (Snow White and the Seven Dwarfs); you could also try your luck with **Alice's Curious Labyrinth** and **'it's a small world'**. Take them for a gentle boat ride round the **Rivers of the Far West**, and visit **Critter Corral** to see some real live animals. Make sure they get a chance to meet **Mickey Mouse** at some point, too. They will probably enjoy **La Cabane des Robinson** (the Swiss Family Robinson Treehouse) and a ride on one of the steam trains. See the shows at **Fantasy Festival Stage**, **Chapparal Theatre** or **Le Théâtre du Château** (the Castle Theatre). Also, catch the daytime parade, even if you do not want to keep the children up late enough to see Main Street, U.S.A. Electrical Parade (on certain dates through the year).

Older Children
Boys usually prefer **Frontierland**, **Adventureland**, and **Discoveryland**, so go to them when you have seen the castle. After a few rides they may want to try absolutely everything, even 'baby rides' like **Dumbo the Flying Elephant** and **Le Carrousel de Lancelot** (Lancelot's Carousel), but they may scorn **Fantasyland's** younger appeal at first.

A Spot of Adrenalin
Frontierland attractions include a runaway mine train at **Big Thunder Mountain** and a visit

to **Phantom Manor**. Have a go shooting bank robbers at the **Rustler Roundup Shootin' Gallery** (you will need extra euros for this). In Adventureland try the rope and plank bridges, and **Indiana Jones™ and the Temple of Peril: Backwards**. In Discoveryland go for maximum throttle in a 'car of the future' on **Autopia** (the race-track), pilot a spaceship in **Orbitron**, or take a ride through outer space in **Star Tours** and **Space Mountain**. Volunteer for **Honey, I Shrunk the Audience**, an amazing shrinking experience with spine-chilling visual and tactile effects. In the evening, be sure to catch the fireworks (seasonal only). The last few seconds are extremely exciting. (See also **Contra-indications** below).

Contra-indications

- No children under three are allowed to ride on **Big Thunder Mountain** and **Star Tours**; none under one on **Dumbo the Flying Elephant**, **Orbitron** and **Casey Jr – le Petit Train de Cirque**). There are height restrictions on **Big Thunder Mountain**, **Indiana Jones™ and the Temple of Peril: Backwards**, **Space Mountain**, **Star Tours** and **Autopia** in Disneyland® Park and on **Rock'n' Roller Coaster starring Aerosmith** in Walt Disney Studios® Park.
- If you suffer from motion

Disney characters add fun to any visit

sickness you may be better off avoiding **Big Thunder Mountain**, **Space Mountain**, **Orbitron** and the **Mad Hatter's Tea Cups**, (and **Rock'n'Roller Coaster** in Walt Disney Studios®) though an excess of ice cream is usually more to blame for the queasiness. **Le Visionarium** can also be mildly disturbing, as the pictures on the screen give a convincing illusion of motion. **Honey, I Shrunk the Audience** is fairly loud and intense.

- If you are pregnant, or have a weak back, heart or neck, avoid jolting rides.

Enjoy a ride on Lancelot's Carousel

What to See

The Essential rating system:

✓ 'top ten'

◆◆◆ do not miss
◆◆ see if you can
◆ worth seeing if you have time

DISNEYLAND® PARK

MAIN STREET, U.S.A.

The scene is set by the flamboyant Victorian splendour of the **Disneyland® Hotel** straddling the entrance gates, even before you pass through the turnstiles into **Station Plaza**. Once visitors emerge into **Town Square** from **Main Street Station**, they are in small-town America at about the turn of the 20th century (as those of us who never saw it like to imagine it might have been). It is a world of gas-lamps and horse-drawn streetcars, decorative lettering and absurdly pretty architecture, all in the colours of Italian ice cream. Each minutely detailed façade in Town Square and Main Street, U.S.A. is different, but the ornate balustrades and bargeboards, pediments and parapets seem to be in perfect scale and harmony. This is a magnificent piece of deception by the Disney Imagineers – the top storeys are subtly graduated in size, so that the castle appears much further away than it really is. All the

Travel by horse-drawn streetcar

street furniture – lamp-posts, letter-boxes, litter-bins, fire hydrants – have been carefully designed to suit the period. Main Street, U.S.A. is the orientation centre of the Theme Park, where you can ask for information, store belongings, hire wheelchairs or pushchairs, book guided tours, find out about lost property (or lost people), and generally warm to the Disneyland® Park mood as marching bands keep up a brisk tempo. The rest of Main Street is mostly devoted to shops and eating places. In **Town Square** there are neat municipal gardens, park benches and a gazebo, where you can wait for one of the trundling period vehicles to take you down Main Street, U.S.A, this links Town Square with the hub of the Theme Park, **Central Plaza**, beside which **Sleeping Beauty Castle** stands. From here you can choose which of the lands to see next. If you prefer, you can take a train from Main Street Station, located up steps just inside Town Square, and either go on a complete circuit of the Theme Park to get your bearings, or get off at Frontierland, Fantasyland or Discoveryland.

Main Street, U.S.A. is popular with vehicle enthusiasts

WHAT TO SEE

ARCADES

There are two covered passageways on either side of Main Street, U.S.A. with rear access to the shops and restaurants. Inside they are beautifully decorated in *fin-de-siècle* style, with wrought-iron work and pretty gas lamps. **Liberty Arcade**, on the left side of Main Street, U.S.A. as you face the castle, contains an exhibition about the Statue of Liberty, with plans, drawings, photographs and the **Statue of Liberty Tableau**. This is a diorama about the unveiling of the monument – a diplomatic touch by Disney, emphasising Franco- American friendship and collaboration. The inaugural ceremony took place in New York harbour in 1886. The 108ft- (33m) high statue by the French sculptor Frédéric-Auguste Bartholdi is made up of bronze strips fixed to a steel frame

The Liberty Arcade is home to the Statue of Liberty exhibition

designed by Gustave Eiffel, who made the headlines barely three years later when his famous tower was inaugurated for the 1889 World Exhibition. 'Liberty enlightening the World' was a gift from the French people to the American people to celebrate the centenary of the American War of Independence and French involvement in it. **Discovery Arcade**, on the right side of Main Street, U.S.A. has cabinets showing various inventions from the early 20th century – flying machines, strange sporting equipment and so on. Fun to look at if you have lots of time.

DISNEYLAND® RAILROAD

These charming steam engines chug around the perimeter of the Theme Park, stopping at Main Street, U.S.A., Frontierland Depot, and Fantasyland and Discoveryland stations. Disneyland® Park would not be complete without an old train or two, for nostalgic railways were one of Walt's abiding passions. He even had a complete track with scaled-down steam engine and carriages built in his garden! At Disneyland® Park there are four individual, authentically styled locomotives, all beautifully painted and fitted and evoking the great railroad days of late-19th-century America. One is a **Presidential Train** of the type used by government officials, another a pioneering **Wild West Train**, the third an **East**

Coast Excursion Train. The fourth is called ***Eureka*** as a reminder of the famous cry which echoed throughout America in 1849 and started the Gold Rush. The engines were manufactured by Welsh boilermakers with every detail carefully in place: whistles, smoke-stacks, cowcatchers and shiny brass fittings. These engines genuinely run on steam produced by water going through a diesel boiler, a departure from authenticity deliberately made by the pollution-conscious Disney team. Each engine fills up with

water from the Frontierland tank every hour or so. The carriages are open on one side, giving good views of the Park. Each train can take about 270 passengers, and one arrives about every 10 minutes; it takes 20 minutes to go right round the Theme Park.

If you prefer buses to trains, take a trip down Memory Lane on a Main Street, U.S.A. omnibus

On the journey between Main Street Station and Frontierland Depot the train passes through **Grand Canyon Diorama** (see page 45).

◆◆◆
THE DISNEY PARADE AND MAIN STREET ELECTRICAL PARADE ✓

The Disney parades are a major attraction and a real focal point of Main Street, U.S.A. They are elaborate, colourful spectacles like carnival processions, with lots of floats. They start near Fantasyland and proceed down Main Street, U.S.A.

Tips

- Main Street Station is generally very busy, so join the Disneyland® Railroad at one of the other stations instead (in Frontierland, Fantasyland or Discoveryland).
- If you are particularly keen to see any attraction, restaurant or show, check at City Hall that it is available.
- Riding a streetcar is a good way of avoiding temptation in **Boardwalk Candy Palace**.
- Do not become mesmerised by all the shops and balloon-sellers unless you have plenty of time. If you spend too long on them, you will not have time to see the rest of the Theme Park.
- Do not let children eat too many sweets before they go on rides.
- If it is raining, head for the arcades at either side of Main Street, U.S.A.
- You can steal a march on the queues by arriving early and walking from Main Street, U.S.A. to **Discoveryland**. Then head for popular attractions before everyone else arrives.

You will find the area very crowded. Stake out a good vantage point in advance. If you time a visit to **Walt's – an American Restaurant** very carefully and are lucky enough to get a window table (very expensive, though) you should get a good view of the parades from the upper floor. Views from the other Main Street, U.S.A. restaurants are distant, or will probably be blocked by kerb-side spectators, but you may be lucky in Plaza Gardens. Disney Theme Parks are famous for their parades. Disneyland® Park's change regularly. The **ImagiNations Parade**, running through 2000,

Enjoy the spectacle of a colourful Disney parade

was the biggest, most imaginative parade yet, featuring huge floats four storeys high. The **Wonderful World of Disney Parade** takes place daily at 3pm, on a more or less regular basis – except when the Christmas Parade takes over with a special guest from Lapland! It is a classic Disney Parade bringing to life scenes from everyone's favourite animated films. Clowns, jugglers, costumed dancers and Disney Characters liven up the procession by fooling around among the crowd and enticing young children to join them.

By night the spectacle is even more remarkable. The **Main Street Electrical Parade**, adopted from Disney Theme Parks in America, contains over one million light bulbs, winking and glowing as night falls in the Theme Park. This parade is definitely worth catching, as it includes some wonderful creations, such as Alice sitting on top of her magic mushroom, and Elliot, a docile dragon, snorting steam at admirers.

As if all this is not enough, the evening's entertainment sometimes ends with a remarkable fireworks display. Guests should note that both the Main Street Electrical Parade and fireworks display are seasonal only.

◆

VEHICLES

Other modes of transportation available in Main Street, U.S.A. date from the same era as the

Main Street Electrical Parade in all its Christmas glory

trains. These vehicles are not genuine antiques, but they are authentically recreated by master craftsmen. Among them are **Horse-Drawn Streetcars** pulled by patient Shires and Percherons (a nod to the French here – it is a local breed), an early double-decker **Omnibus**, a chauffeured **Limousine**, a **Fire Truck** and a police **Paddy Wagon**. Guests can queue up in Town Square for a brief ride to Central Plaza in whichever vehicle is running. But don't be deceived by **Main Street Motors**, which, in spite of its name and the reconditioned genuine vintage car on display inside, sells souvenirs based on Disney and animated films.

FRONTIERLAND

This is the largest of the five lands, distinguished from the others by a Wild West theme, large expanses of water, and a spectacular Arizona-style landscape. Here there is one of the Theme Park's most exciting attractions, **Big Thunder Mountain**, and two different kinds of boat trip are offered. Like Main Street, U.S.A., Frontierland has a clear architectural theme, based on an imaginary Wild West town of the late 1800s called Thunder Mesa. If parts of Frontierland look surprisingly authentic, that is because they are. Disney Imagineers collected real antiques from many states in the US, and transported them here for special effect.

There is something for everyone at Frontierland. Even if you are not a Wild West enthusiast, you will almost certainly be impressed by the drama of this entirely artificial landscape, created from flat, unpromising terrain. The Disney Imagineers excelled themselves here, recreating the vastness of the American West to such an extent that, looking at the wild canyons and ochre-coloured sandstone monoliths, you will imagine yourself travelling through the Rocky Mountains. Pioneer fever will no doubt grip you as you step into the Lucky Nugget Saloon to have a meal and watch a real French cancan show!

The Lucky Nugget restaurant

Tips

- If it is raining you can walk under cover to Frontierland, from Liberty Arcade in Main Street, U.S.A. or from the Adventureland Bazaar.
- **Big Thunder Mountain** and (to a lesser extent) **Phantom Manor** are major attractions where queues are likely to be long, so try to visit them early, late, or at meal or parade times.
- If the weather is hot, head for the paddlewheel steamboats or River Rogue Keelboats.

You can approach Frontierland from several directions. The usua way is from Central Plaza, throug **Fort Comstock**, the log stockade If you are going around the Park anti-clockwise, you can approacl Frontierland from Adventureland and watch how cleverly the pirat scene fades to cowboys and Indians. You can also come by train (they chug clockwise round the Theme Park). On the way between Main Street Station and Frontierland Depot, trains pass through **Grand Canyon Diorama**

Big Thunder Mountain is at the heart of Frontierland

WHAT TO SEE

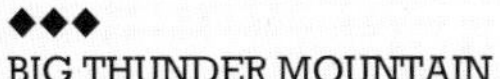

◆◆◆ BIG THUNDER MOUNTAIN ✓

The most exciting and conspicuous attraction in Frontierland, and certainly one of the best in Disneyland® Park. It may take a little while to pluck up enough courage to visit it, so wild are the screams from those riding it. But do not miss it. It is reached by taking a roller-coaster ride aboard a runaway mine train. The track passes through a carefully reconstructed landscape, similar to that found in Arizona or Utah, particularly around Monument Valley. The rocky set rises to 119 feet (36m), and immense pains have been taken to achieve an impression of age in the mine buildings, by means of staining, bleaching and rusting.

The ride is certainly wilder than at Orlando. What makes the former so good is its mystery factor. Unlike most roller-coasters, the runaway mine train at Big Thunder Mountain is unpredictable and once the train goes into the mine-workings anything can happen.

Even the queuing is creatively arranged for this attraction – the tightly coiled lines shuffle steadily through the extremely realistic reconstruction of the Big Thunder Mountain Mining Company's headquarters. Tension builds up as the point of no return is reached. The train pulls away, then plunges into a shaft and the caverns of the mine-workings, full of stalactites and glowing bats' eyes. Hurtling through a mining camp and a pine-forest, where opossoms swing from the branches, the train then dives into a dynamite explosion. The roof caves in, briefly revealing huge veins of gold. The train plunges on, this time facing a new danger from the flooding river, which is washing away part of the track. Eventually the

Big Thunder Mountain is not for the faint-hearted!

exhilarated passengers are brought safely back to base, chortling with delight, eager to do it all again.

This popular attraction is certainly one that can stand a repeat performance, as it is difficult to take in all the details in one go. Children under three (or below a certain height) are not allowed to go on the ride; nor should anyone consider going on it if they are pregnant, or have neck or back problems.

◆

CRITTER CORRAL

Enclosure of a typical Western ranch near Frontierland Depot (railway station) where visitors can see and pet some real animals of an unthreatening nature.

FORT COMSTOCK AND LEGENDS OF THE WILD WEST

Guarding the main entrance to Frontierland, Fort Comstock is a replica of the sort of log stockade constructed by early pioneers as a defence against Indian attack. Inside a series of picturesque scenes depict life in the American West with the help of legendary types of characters immortalised in famous westerns; there is the gold prospector called 'Forty-Niner', because of the 1849 Gold Rush, the outlaw, the lawman, as well as the larger than life characters, Buffalo Bill and Davy Crockett.

The Indian Camp outside gives a vivid account of the Native Americans' traditional way of life and visitors can admire authentic Cheyenne handicraft. The tour also offers a splendid overall view of Frontierland and the opportunity to meet a real Cheyenne Indian chief.

◆

GRAND CANYON DIORAMA

Although this attraction is located within Frontierland, it can only be seen from the **Disneyland® Railroad** (trains depart regularly from Main Street, U.S.A., Frontierland, Fantasyland and Discoveryland stations).

Trains enter a 262foot (80m) tunnel, in which the scenery of the Grand Canyon is recreated, subtly lit to give the impression that the journey along the canyon rim takes not just a few minutes, but an entire day from sunrise to sunset. Guests first encounter ancient Indian cliff dwellings hollowed from the canyon walls, and then a forest in which a herd of deer is grazing. Other wildlife can be seen, too: a fox stalking a pack rat; a rattlesnake coiled on a ledge; raccoons and squirrels; and a cougar and her cubs by a cave. A thunderstorm gathers and, as a rainbow forms, antelope descend into the canyon. The diorama consists of a huge mural, with many animals and species of vegetation. Lighting, music and sound effects all play a part. As the train emerges from the tunnel passengers find they have reached the **Rivers of the Far West**, with **Big Thunder Mountain** beyond.

◆◆◆
PHANTOM MANOR ✓

The eerie, ramshackle mansion of Phantom Manor was built by one of Thunder Mesa's early settlers, who became rich during the Gold Rush. But tragedy struck when his only daughter disappeared on her wedding day. The house was left empty and fell into decay. You can believe this if you like – but isn't that a candle inside? Guests bound for Phantom Manor are ushered into a strange circular room by sinister hosts. The doors shut and the walls change shape. Those innocent-looking pictures take on horrifying new dimensions as the floor stretches. Guests then descend to board a 'Doom Buggy' for the journey through the house. Mocking laughter, beating door-knockers, creaking hinges, and a clock tolling 13 start the mystery tour. A ghostly bride appears sobbing at intervals, while a medium's head is visible in a crystal ball. One of the best special effects is the holograms, which are used for the wedding feast. Guests dance and fade, and a parade of ghosts, ghouls and skeletons follows before the passengers are released from their ordeal.

Outside in the fresh air, guests emerge near **Boot Hill**, the cemetery overlooking the Rivers of the Far West, which is full of amusing gravestones. Some are even, by Disney standards, slightly *risqué*: 'Sacred to the Memory of Rev. Jared Bates, who died Aug 6 1862. Erected by the girls of The Lucky Nugget Saloon'.

All sorts of spooks haunt Phantom Manor

◆◆
RIVER ROGUE KEELBOATS (RACCOON AND COYOTE)

These boats are modelled on the ones used in a Disney television film called *Davy Crockett and the River Pirates.* They are diesel-powered, 40 feet (12m) long and hold about 40 passengers each. Unlike the stately paddlewheel riverboats, which follow a fixed course, the keelboats weave in and out, and you may find yourself perilously close to the rocks at some point. The keelboats leave from a dock at **Smuggler's Cove** (subject to weather conditions).

Stately paddlewheel riverboats like the Molly Brown *(right), ply the Rivers of the Far West on their nostalgic voyages*

MOLLY BROWN

◆

RUSTLER ROUNDUP SHOOTIN' GALLERY

This is fun. Instead of bullets, the guns fire electronic impulses at a Wild West scene containing 74 animated targets: among them cacti, a windmill and a dynamite shack. (The only human one is a peeping Tom.) If you hit them, all kinds of things happen. There is a charge for this attraction to prevent people from hogging the guns all day.

◆◆

THUNDER MESA RIVERBOAT LANDING (PADDLEWHEEL RIVERBOATS)

The careful landscaping and detailing of the various sections of the **Rivers of the Far West** make the paddlewheel riverboat trip round **Big Thunder Mountain** quite an adventure. On the way you will see **Smuggler's Cove**; **Wilderness Island**, a green oasis where Joe sleeps in a rocking-chair, his dog barking at passing boats; **Settlers' Landing**, a dry dock with supplies for pioneering homesteaders; an abandoned wagon with two skeletal oxen in the sand; and **Geyser Plateau**, where steaming, bubbling, mineral-rich water jets over the bones of dinosaurs. The scenery evokes the landscape of the Wild West, with its grand geological formations (rock bridges and canyons) and high desert plateaux known as *mesas*. From Thunder Mesa Riverboat Landing near the **Silver Spur Steakhouse** visitors can choose between two

Boot Hill, a place of rest in Frontierland

riverboats: *Mark Twain* and *Molly Brown*. They are both authentically reconstructed paddlewheel riverboats of the type that plied the Mississippi and Sacramento rivers at the time of the Gold Rush. One is a stern-wheeler, the other a side-wheeler. They were both built specifically for Disneyland® Park. The vessels are ornately fitted with mahogany and brass, with teak decks and comfortable upholstery. Each boat carries about 400 passengers, and their nostalgic voyage lasts around 15 minutes.

ADVENTURELAND

This is one of the most attractive parts of Disneyland® Park. In contrast to Frontierland, here there is no geographic unity since the inspiration of the Disney Imagineers was drawn from three continents – the islands of the Caribbean, the African desert and the Asian jungle. Yet Adventureland looks pleasantly landscaped in a natural style, with water, islands, rocks and lots of vegetation, including a bamboo grove. In addition, it has two of the most popular rides, a collection of genuinely interesting shops in its North African bazaar, and several of the nicest eating places. In all, it has a lot going for it, and should appeal to any age group. One of the two main attractions, **Pirates of the Caribbean**, is complex and technically sophisticated – yet Adventureland as a whole has an air of innocence about it in keeping with the original spirit of Disney. Its pleasures are simpler than much of the Theme Park – climbing treehouses, walking wobbly bridges, exploring caves. The central physical feature is **Adventure Isle**, a moated double-island connected by two exciting bridges. Skilful landscaping gives this area the impression of being larger than it really is. Elements from three well-known Disney movies are incorporated into the themes here: *Peter Pan*, *Treasure Island* and *Swiss Family Robinson*.

The exotic entrance to Adventureland

WHAT TO SEE

ADVENTURE ISLE

The north section of Adventure Isle is given over to a pirate theme. The Jolly Roger flies by the lookout tower on **Spyglass Hill**. Below is **Ben Gunn's Cave**, with six different entrances: **Dead Man's Maze**, **Davy Jones's Locker**, and so on, leading to mysterious passages haunted by bats and skeletons. Waterfalls hurtle past gaps in the rock, shaped like an enormous skull. **Captain Hook's Pirate Ship** is moored in the cove nearby, and you can walk over the top deck to spy out the land. Down below, light snacks are served from the galley. At night **Skull Rock** and the waterfalls are illuminated. They look most eerie.

LA CABANE DES ROBINSON (THE SWISS FAMILY ROBINSON TREEHOUSE)

Prominent on **Adventure Isle** is a strange-looking artificial banyan (fig) tree, rising 91feet (28m). In its branches, bearing 300,000 leaves and 50,000 flowers, is the ultimate treehouse, where the resourceful Robinson family have made a home from shipwrecked timbers. Wooden stairways lead to various rooms, while down by the roots of the tree is **le Ventre de la Terre**, where supplies from the wreck are stored behind bamboo bars. (The actual wreck can be seen under the suspended bridge.)

INDIANA JONES™ AND THE TEMPLE OF PERIL: BACKWARDS ✓

This is a daring high-speed roller coaster ride culminating in a thrilling loop the loop experience. We all know the fearless archaeologist whose adventures have been the subject of several exciting films. The setting here is an ancient temple full of hidden treasures, all in a wild, untamed jungle. Aboard a goldmine cart you begin a perilous chase up, over and under the mine site, past

A rope and plank bridge leads to Adventure Isle

ancient statues and teetering columns. And if that isn't enough to get the adrenalin flowing, the ride is backwards all the way.

◆◆
LE PASSAGE ENCHANTÉ D'ALADDIN (ALADDIN'S ENCHANTED WORLD)

Situated in **Adventureland Bazaar**, this attraction brings to life the enchanted city of Aladdin's tales. As you walk through an Arabian Nights décor, various scenes from *Aladdin* appear before your eyes, with animated figures and special light and sound effects which help to carry you on the wings of your imagination from the city of Agrabah to the Cave of Wonders where the magic lamp lies hidden.

◆◆◆
PIRATES OF THE CARIBBEAN ✓

One of the block-busting attractions of the park, a must for everyone. There are similar attractions at the other Disney theme parks, too, but here the latest *Audio-Animatronics®* technology is employed, giving an even wider range of special effects. As you make your way through the rocky grotto to the boats, you can hear roistering buccaneers singing their favourite song. You are about to embark on a time-travel

Pirate enthusiasts can eat lunch on Captain Hook's Galley

adventure, going back to a 17th-century scene somewhere in the West Indies, where palms wave and the air is warm and balmy. The boat sets off through the moonlit **Blue Lagoon** and gradually the sounds of distant gunfire grow louder; a fortress is being shelled by a pirate ship. Pirates are attempting to scale the walls, daggers clutched between their teeth. The boat then passes inside the fortress. The prisoners in the dungeons call for help. Suddenly, the boat plunges down a waterfall and returns to the battle scene. Cannon balls and smoke are everywhere. The voyage continues through the centre of a Caribbean town, and here the ride is so packed with detailed scenery that it is hard to take everything in amid the general plunder and mayhem (none of it frightening or violent). The fort's burning arsenal explodes, propelling passengers back to the present and the final stage of the ride. Passengers can buy pirate souvenirs afterwards in **Le Coffre du Capitaine**.

As many as 124 *Audio-Animatronics*® figures are used, including animals. Some of the animated scenes are highly naturalistic and sophisticated: full of sword-fights, facial gestures and so on. The weapons are authentic replicas of 16th- and 17th-century pieces. The dialogue is mostly in colloquial French, but clues are almost entirely visual, so there is no great loss of enjoyment for non-French speakers. This ride is so action-packed that you could certainly do it more than once.

FANTASYLAND

When you reach the neat gardens and fountains of Central Plaza, you can see straight ahead of you the mysterious gilded pinnacles of a truly fantastic castle, and the drawbridge is down, just waiting for you to cross.
Sleeping Beauty Castle is the main landmark of Disneyland® Park. It is slap in the centre and unmissable, so it is always a good place to meet. As the spires can be seen from most sections of the Park, they can give bearings if you get lost.
If you approach Fantasyland from Central Plaza when the live show is on at the open-air Théâtre du Château at the foot of the castle, take time to watch as it will put you and your children in the right mood for the fairy-tale world you are about to enter. You would be surprised how many adults enjoy themselves watching Winnie the Pooh and friends too! (selected dates April/May–September). These shows are renewed regularly but are always very popular.
There is another live show in Fantasy Festival Stage, near Fantasyland Station.
Most of Fantasyland's attractions are designed for younger guests; teenagers may find **Dumbo the Flying Elephant** a little beneath their dignity. At first, that is.
The theme of Fantasyland, as its name suggests, is the world of fairytales: witches and dwarfs, princes and princesses, gingerbread houses and magic wishing wells. The European origin of these fairytales is heavily emphasised. Architecture ranges from quaint, Bavarian-looking cottages to the ambitious medieval whimsy of the castle itself.
Several of the attractions are

Fairytale Land

similar in type: short rides through enclosed spaces, during which a fairy story is unfurled with many elaborate sets and moving figures. The characters are deliberately based on Disney animated films. There is no attempt to make them look like 'real people'. Queues for these attractions are lengthy. **Les Voyages de Pinocchio** (Pinocchio's Travels) or **Peter Pan's Flight** are difficult to follow if you are not already familiar with the stories, though you can still enjoy the rides. Other attractions are of the fair-ground variety – in the form of classic merry-go-rounds and a few mild G-forces. If you know other Disney Theme Parks you will probably remember the block-busting and eternally popular **'it's a small world'**, here given more elaboration. Completely new attractions are the hedge maze of **Alice's Curious Labyrinth** – again, a strongly European feature, and **Le Pays de Contes de Fées** (Fairytale Land).

Elsewhere in Fantasyland there are many shops selling toys and sweets, and there are also lots of fairytale eating places (designed mostly with children in mind), including one of the few restaurants in the Theme Park with French cuisine. You can reach Fantasyland by the **Disneyland® Railroad**, but after that you must use your feet.

Tips

- Catch the fantasy attractions when queues are short if you can – early or late in the day, or during meal-times and parades, when crowds will be thinner.
- Get a Fastpass ticket for Peter Pan's Flight as soon as you arrive in Fantasyland. It is a very popular ride with extremely long queues.
- Very young or susceptible children may find parts of **Blanche-Neige et les Sept Nains** (Snow White and the Seven Dwarfs), **La Tanière du Dragon** (The Dragon's Lair) and **Peter Pan's Flight** frightening.
- Check show times at **Le Théâtre du Château** or the **Fantasy Festival Stage** when you arrive.
- You may have an expensive time if you let your children investigate too many of the shops.

WHAT TO SEE

◆◆

ALICE'S CURIOUS LABYRINTH

Based, of course, on *Alice in Wonderland*, this maze of clipped yew and ivy hedges is 1,200 feet (366m) long. The visitor passes characters and scenes from *Alice*: the Cheshire Cat, which rolls its eyes and twitches its tail, a blue caterpillar calmly smoking a hookah, strange birds and, of course, the choleric Queen of Hearts advocating decapitation at every turn. Eventually you reach a small purple castle, full of optical illusions. The jumping fountains transfix passers-by; arcs of water leap from pool to pool round the edge of the

Sleeping Beauty Castle

Alice's Curious Labyrinth

maze. The designs for some parts of this attraction are unusual and keep children amused for quite some time.

◆

BLANCHE-NEIGE ET LES SEPT NAINS (SNOW WHITE AND THE SEVEN DWARFS)

Climb aboard the diamond-mine cars outside the Dwarfs' cottage, and set off through this German fairytale, on which Walt Disney based one of his most successful animated films. The wicked queen does her stuff with the mirror and the poisoned apple, and Prince Charming appears at the end.

LE CARROUSEL DE LANCELOT (LANCELOT'S CAROUSEL)

A classic merry-go-round, with 86 ornate, medieval war horses trotting through fairytale scenes. An enjoyable, gentle ride.

◆◆

CASEY JR – LE PETIT TRAIN DU CIRQUE (THE LITTLE CIRCUS TRAIN)

Straight out of the Disney classic *Dumbo* this circus train rides up and down small hills and over bridges as it jerks its passengers swiftly round the miniature sets of Le Pays des Contes de Fées (Fairytale Land – see separate entry on page 59). A gentle ride that the whole family will enjoy.

Dumbo, a star attraction

◆◆

DUMBO THE FLYING ELEPHANT

The long queues for this ride testify to the popular appeal of this simple roundabout for young children. You can control the height at which your elephant flies.

◆◆◆ SLEEPING BEAUTY CASTLE ✓

This is the archetypal interpretation of a castle – one we instantly recognise from the pages of any storybook, or from early Disney movies, such as the animated classic *Sleeping Beauty*. The design is based on illustrations from a 17th-century edition of *Les Très Riches Heures du Duc de Berry*, and the building rises 149 feet (45.5m) above the moat. A technique known as 'forced perspective' has been employed, to give an illusion of even greater height. The pink walls are topped by 16 whimsical ornamental turrets of subtle, sea-blue tiles. Pennants, weather vanes and golden finials adorn the roofline; creepers hang from the walls; and enticing stairways lead to the central tower. Visitors can enter the castle by the drawbridge, or from the side by the wishing well (**Le Puits Magique**); do not forget to wish. Once inside, turn and look up at the front window – and wait a few seconds. Magically, its design will transform from two doves into a rose. This is a 'polage window', and it works by means of a rotating filter. Upstairs, in **la Galerie de la Belle au Bois Dormant** (Sleeping Beauty's Gallery) there is an exhibition of hand-woven Aubusson tapestries, colourful stained-glass windows made by English craftsmen and illuminated manuscripts depicting the famous story of Sleeping Beauty. From the balcony, the view over Fantasyland is splendid.

◆◆◆ 'it's a small world'

Like similar attractions at Tokyo, Orlando and Anaheim, this is a very popular and elaborate entertainment. In Disneyland® Park it is a fantastic amalgam of many different architectural landmarks, ranging from Big Ben to the Leaning Tower of Pisa. The set is constructed in miniature.

Pinocchio meets the crowds

Every quarter of an hour a parade of animated figures troops around the base of the clocktower, and many exciting things happen before you are eventually told what time it is. Guests can have a ride in canal boats past a gathering of *Audio-Animatronics*® 'children' from all parts of the globe. Norwegian figure-skaters give way to leprechauns, London's Beefeaters, Flamenco dancers, Balinese fan-dancers, and the like.

It is a saccharine show, but the technical effects are nonetheless impressive. There are nearly 280 different figures, representing a phenomenal effort by the Disney costume department.

MAD HATTER'S TEA CUPS

A pleasantly loony whirl in 18 giant tea cups, placed on a roundabout, resulting in a bewildering pirouette of motion. You control the speed using a steering wheel.

LE PAYS DES CONTES DE FÉES (FAIRYTALE LAND)

Miniature scenes from European fairy tales unfold slowly as children of all ages take a canal cruise through familiar landscapes that recreate the magical appeal of delightful tales such as Hansel and Gretel, the Little Mermaid or Beauty and the Beast. But there is more...the imposing Mount Olympus where Greek gods once lived, Aladdin's cave and the legend of King Arthur.

PETER PAN'S FLIGHT 

Pirate galleons 'sail' over the rooftops of London to Never Land, giving an illusion of flight. A delightful journey for day-dreamers of all ages.

LES PIROUETTES DU VIEUX MOULIN (TWIRLING OLD MILL)

An old windmill is the setting of this big wheel attraction which offers a good overall view of Fantasyland.

LA TANIÈRE DU DRAGON (THE DRAGON'S LAIR)

Chained by the neck in a dark cave of bubbling pools and stalactites is a leathery grey dragon, wonderfully terrifying. It makes gentle snorings and twitchings, then flashes its red eyes and gives fierce roars, smoke pouring from its nostrils. Its tail lashes in the water, while the wings move and claws tense. It is one of the most remarkable and sophisticated pieces of *Audio-Animatronics*® technology in the Theme Park. You can reach the lair from the mysterious shop called **Merlin l'Enchanteur**, carved into the rock of the castle.

LES VOYAGES DE PINOCCHIO (PINOCCHIO'S TRAVELS)

Based on the story told by Carlo Collodi. The cars pass from cheery Alpine landscapes into dangers and temptations, and then emerge back in Geppetto's shop, where the clockwork toys spring to life.

DISCOVERYLAND

This European version of Tomorrowland also looks back at the great inventors and visionaries of the past. Here, in France, Jules Verne is given a prominent role; H G Wells and Leonardo da Vinci are also featured. Travel through time and space, science fiction, special effects and speed form the basis of the two shows (**Le Visionarium** and **Videopolis**), and six attractions you will probably have to queue for: **Star Tours**, **Autopia**, **Orbitron**, **Les Mystères du Nautilus** (The Mystery of the Nautilus), **Honey, I Shrunk the Audience**, and **Space Mountain**.

If, as many people do, you tackle the Theme Park clockwise, this is the last land you will come to, and psychologically it feels as though it should be. The architecture is futuristic, with lights and flashing lasers.

WHAT TO SEE

AUTOPIA

This is a popular attraction, consisting of a ride in a 'Car of the Future' through 'Solaria', a city of tomorrow. Your car is

Tips

- If you feel like sitting down, time your meal at **Café Hyperion** during the **Videopolis** show.
- Check the entertainment programme for times

Rolling up to be shrunk at Honey, I Shrunk the Audience

The Nautilus is as surprising inside as out

kept firmly on a specific track, and all you have to do is press the accelerator and steer.

◆◆◆
HONEY, I SHRUNK THE AUDIENCE ✓

This original attraction, inspired by the two Disney success *Honey, I Shrunk the Kids* and *Honey, I Blew up the Kid*, opened to great acclaim in 1999. You watch as accident-prone inventor Wayne Szalinski (hero of the two films) demonstrates his shrinking and enlarging machine and commits his biggest blunder – pointing the machine at the audience! From the start you are carefully prepared for the worst as you are given special glasses to wear as you enter the first auditorium, where a multimedia pre-show whets the appetite. You are then ushered into the main auditorium and the action starts, as state of the art special effects create the highly convincing 'shrinking' effect, through 3D visual effects, surround sound and touch sensations on leg and face. The show reaches its height when young Adam Szalinski picks up the auditorium and the whole theatre starts to shake…

◆◆◆
LES MYSTÈRES DU NAUTILUS (THE MYSTERY OF THE NAUTILUS)

This attraction was inspired by Disney's movie *20,000 Leagues under the Sea* based on Jules Verne's novel. Docked in Discoveryland's lagoon, the Nautilus is Captain Nemo's submarine, the strange universe of an eccentric visionary who plays the organ at the bottom of the sea. An undersea passage, reached through a nearby lighthouse, leads to the interior of the submarine.

The tour of the vessel holds a few surprises in store for you as well as some spine-chilling sound and light effects. It begins in the Treasure Room and ends in the Engine Room.

Star Tours

ORBITRON

There is nothing new about the basic principle of this ride, but it certainly looks different. Bronze, copper and brass globes spin on various axes, the opposite way from the direction of your two-seater craft, so if you are at maximum height (controlled from inside) it seems quite fast. Queues can be long, as there are only 12 passenger vehicles.

The airship Hyperion *floats over the entrance to Videopolis*

♦♦♦

STAR TOURS

This exciting ride draws on the themes and special effects used in George Lucas's epic adventure, *Star Wars*. As much excitement is created by the build-up as by the ride itself. The sci-fi 'business' before you are actually strapped into your spacecraft, when visitors can watch friendly droids working, is all part of the fun, and certainly takes tedium out of queuing.

The ride is based on a popular comic theme: the novice driver. This one, unfortunately, is your pilot for the space flight. Fasten your seat-belts. The space craft pitches, rolls and jolts, while on-screen, rapidly moving images suggest you are falling or on some irrevocable collision course. Eventually, of course, you land safely to be greeted by Rox-N, a clever robot who presents the interactive computer games of **L'Astroport Services Interstellaires** (Star Tours Post-Show) in five languages. There is an X-ray detector with videoscreen projection to eliminate minute space creatures. There is also a sophisticated camera which takes your photograph and projects it on a large screen; you can then distort it at will by dragging your finger across the screen. But the most exciting game is **Star Course** in which would-be pilots try their skill at avoiding obstacles while hurtling through space at high speed.

♦♦

VIDEOPOLIS

The airship *Hyperion* marks this pavilion, which houses a large tiered **auditorium**, where visitors can enjoy videos relayed on four giant screens and regular live shows. The Café Hyperion offers a good view of the stage, so you can enjoy hamburgers and hotdogs while you watch. These are supported by unearthly special effects created by lasers, lights and artificial mist.

◆◆◆
LE VISIONARIUM (THE VISIONARIUM) ✓

This is an enjoyable production based on the time-travel theme, using the medium known as *Circle-Vision 360®*, which will be familiar to anyone who has visited the Disney Theme Parks in America. In these attractions the audience is completely surrounded by a belt of large cinema screens. The totality of this cinematic experience is achieved by using nine different cameras controlled by computer. Spectacular landscapes, many different perspectives and a very convincing illusion of movement are just some aspects of this entertaining show. In Disney's other Theme Parks *Circle-Vision* films have been mostly confined to tourist travelogues, but here for the first time is a plot. There is a robot inventor called Time-keeper; 9-Eye, a robot with nine cameras around her head (for this creature is female, it seems); and Jules Verne as honorary guest, collected from the Paris Exposition of 1900 for a voyage through time. Gérard Depardieu puts in a brief appearance as an airport baggage handler and Jeremy Irons as HG Wells. The shooting of this film involved some adventures, including sending the expensive nine-camera turret under the sea.

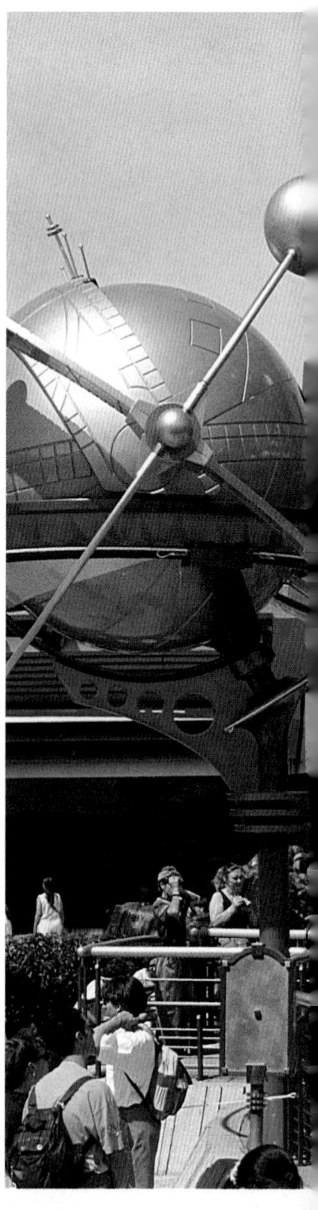

In Discoveryland you can indulge in time travel, or enjoy space travel on rides such as Orbitron (right)

◆◆◆
SPACE MOUNTAIN – DE LA TERRE À LA LUNE (FROM THE EARTH TO THE MOON) ✓

This attraction undoubtedly marks the climax of a visit to the Disneyland® Park, for the setting, the sounds and the awe-inspiring darkness, torn by incandescent asteroids, are all designed to make you feel like pioneers embarking on a unique space adventure.
For space travel volunteers, the exhilarating experience begins long before boarding the rocket ship: while you slowly make your way through the heart of the impressive 118 feet- (36m) high 'mountain', you experience a taste of the dangers ahead with meteorites and explosions all around. The curious but less daring may also enter the mountain and walk along special gangways from which one gets the most vivid impression of this fantastic space journey.
But the count-down to blast off is ticking away and it is time for the rocket ship to enter the barrel of the 72 feet- (22m) long Columbiad Cannon, inspired by Jules Verne's novel *From the Earth to the Moon* published in 1865, over 100 years before man first set foot on the moon. During the catapult launch, which lasts a mere 1.8 seconds, passengers experience an acceleration of 1.3g before plunging into space on a hair-raising half mile (1km) journey at a top speed of 43 miles (70km) per hour. In its efforts to avoid impending annihilation, the rocket ship makes three complete inversion loops while a sophisticated on-board audio system, synchronised with the ride experience, adds to the thrills, if that were still possible.
Compared with other attractions ot a similar type, Space Mountain represents a huge leap forward in innovation and technological precision, which enables a rocket ship to be launched every 36 seconds!

Space Mountain looks even more alien after dark

WALT DISNEY STUDIOS® PARK

Background

The idea of a second European Disney park on the theme of cinema, animation and television goes back to 1992, just before Disneyland® Park opened, but Disney Imagineers were only given the green light to begin planning and designing the new park in 1997; they based their work on the concept of the successful Disney-MGM Studios at Walt Disney World in Florida and adapted their new creation to European audiences with the help of European professionals in the world of cinema, such as Rémy Julienne, the French stunt designer.

A brand new experience

Disneyland® Park brought to life on a grand scale the Disney Characters and Magic that have enchanted several generations of children. The new Walt Disney Studios® Park, opened ten years later, is designed to take its guests to the very source of the Disney magic, on a thrilling interactive journey behind-the-scenes to discover some of the secrets of Disney animation, to marvel at special effects, to witness spectacular stunts and take part in a live television broadcast. And, anything can happen when Mickey takes over as cameraman! Lights on, take one!

Walt Disney Studios Park in figures

- The park was designed by a team of 300 Imagineers
- It covers an area of 62 acres (25ha)
- Its construction required 5,000 tons of stainless steel, 1.5 million cubic feet of cement and 262 miles of radio cabling
- It prompted the creation of 1500 direct and 3,000 indirect jobs
- It is expected to boost the number of visitors to Disneyland Resort Paris to 17 million during the first year
- The water tower, a symbol of Disney Studios, stands 108 feet (33m) high

WHAT TO SEE

The park is divided into four distinct production areas based on a real studio and includes ten attractions and several shops and restaurants. In addition, there is endless entertainment called 'Streetmosphere': actors, musician and characters adding to the atmosphere of a real working film studio.

FRONT LOT

Beyond the park's gates, the inviting courtyard shaded by palm trees with a fountain in its centre (could it be Mickey in disguise?!) reveals none of the excitement that lies ahead. The focal point of this area, known as 'Front Lot' in cinema jargon, is undoubtedly the 108 foot-(33m) tall water tower topped by Mickey's famous pair of black ears. Originally used to fight fires, such towers became the symbol of a Hollywood film studio; this one was modelled on the water tower erected near the entrance to the Disney Studios in Burbank, California in 1939. And as one might expect, there is a definite 1930s air about the place. Beyond the courtyard lies the entrance to Disney Studio 1.

Disney Studio 1

Here you step straight into the glaring lights of a Hollywood film set, Hollywood Boulevard, packed with movie props and lined with shops and a restaurant, where guests become part of the action! Studio 1 is a veiled reference to Walt Disney's studios in Los Angeles, which were the birthplace of the Mickey Mouse animated shorts and of Disney's first full-length animated film, Snow White and the Seven Dwarfs. Some of the sets are inspired by buildings that actually existed, others help to recreate the atmosphere of Hollywood during the first half of the 20th century.

ANIMATION COURTYARD

This is the temple of the art of animation for which the name of Disney became famous worldwide. Three attractions, including exhibits and shows, are devoted to the evolution of animation from its European origins to the most sophisticated feature-length animated pictures of our time.

Art of Disney Animation

When he visited Disneyland® Resort Paris, before the opening of the new Theme Park, Roy Disney, Walt Disney's nephew and Chairman of Walt

A touch of Hollywood in Paris

Disney Feature Animation, was thrilled by this attraction. Creating the illusion of motion is a dream that goes back to Prehistoric Man. Many pioneers have tried to make this dream come true and the pre-show film pays homage to these now-forgotten forerunners. The pre-show area also displays various artefacts, some of them quite unique, such as the multi-plane camera developed by Walt Disney in the 1930s to add depth to animated images by allowing various parts of the same picture to be animated separately. And why not have a go yourself at the 'persistence of vision' apparatus?
The attraction itself, a sequence which takes place in three successive rooms, includes a film with highlights from Disney's animated classics (screened in the Disney Classics Theater), which will whet your appetite for what follows in the second room, Drawn to Animation: a demonstration of how it is done by a Disney artist with the help of Mushu, the little red dragon from the film Mulan. After this, character animation will no longer hold any secret for you and you will be given a chance to try your newly acquired skill at the interactive play stations located in the last room.

Animagique

Staged in a 1,100-seat theatre, this 'black-light' show using giant fluorescent puppets, ultra-violet light and special effects is partly orchestrated by Donald Duck...with strange results as you can imagine! Characters from your favourite Disney animated pictures (Mickey, Donald, Pinocchio, the pink elephants, the whale...) come to life in this three-dimensional animated show...as if by magic!

Flying Carpets Over Agrabah

What happens when Aladdin's Genie is let loose? Illusion and reality become mixed up...all you can do is hang on to your magic carpet, let yourself be whirled round the giant magic lamp and enjoy the experience!

PRODUCTION COURTYARD

A statue of Charlie Chaplin as he appeared in City Lights, one of his most moving films, marks the entrance to this part of Walt Disney Studios® Park. This is the hub of the studios, the place where it all happens, where the spectators' dream becomes reality…on screen!

Television Production Tour

This is now home to the Disney Channel France and it is the very first time that a television network has been based inside a Disney theme park! A tour guide shows guests round the Transmission Centre, from which Disney Channel programmes are broadcast throughout France, as well as round the Pre- and Post Production areas. Live broadcasts, in particular the popular 'Zapping Zone' programme, take place six days a week. Guests can watch the sequence of events from a glass corridor and get a real insight into the workings of a television studio. But that is not all…how about watching yourself appear on TV?

CinéMagique

As the name implies, this show is a tribute to the magic appeal of the European and US cinema over the past hundred years. Featuring a selection of the most exciting film excerpts as well as a review of the actors and actresses who are now part of the legend, it invites guests to relive the cinema's greatest moments. Inside the 1,100-seat theatre, do not be deceived by the 1930s decor. The latest technology is here…you are about to experience its powerful effects and witness a disconcerting but exciting fusion between fiction and reality!

Try a career in modelling

Studio Tram Tour featuring Catastrophe Canyon

If you think this is just a tourist ride round the production area with a chance to see what goes on behind the scenes….you're right….well not quite!
Film sets, props, special effects, decors and costumes will hold no secrets for you when you come out, but there is one mighty detail which will make all the difference to your flow of adrenaline: your tram will take a detour via Catastrophe Canyon and from then on it's all hell let loose as you find yourself at the heart of the special-effect shooting of a series of hair-raising disasters! This is bound to be one of the most popular attractions in Walt Disney Studios® Park and guests are advised to make use of the Fastpass Service (see page 30).

BACKLOT

According to studio jargon, this area is usually not on show… this is where the tricks of the trade are developed, perfected and eventually filmed, all very hush-hush and definitely out of

Disaster strikes in Catastrophe Canyon

bounds, but not at Walt Disney Studios® Park!

Armageddon, Special Effects

This attraction takes its name from the American science-fiction film featuring the Mir space station. The pre-show area pays tribute to the inventor of special effects, Frenchman George Méliès, and puts you in the mood for what is in store for you! Once you step on board the space station, the mounting suspense becomes almost unbearable as all sorts of apocalyptic things happen…or do they? Could it be that those visual and sound effects are more real than reality itself? Well the thrill is real enough anyway, so enjoy it!

Rock'n'Roller Coaster starring Aerosmith

A spine-chilling ride with a difference! It has the speed, the acceleration, the loops, the turns, the drops that you'd expect…but it also has the music and stunning visual effects! What more could you ask for?

Make use of the Fastpass service to reduce waiting time at this attraction (see page 30).

Stunt Show Spectacular

This is what every James Bond fan would like to see…a live stunt show! And this is exactly what Walt Disney Studios® Park is offering you, a breathtaking spectacular staged up to five times a day in a 3,000-seat outdoor arena. The scene is a seaside village in southern France, the action: a live shooting of various stunts with purpose-designed powerful cars, motorbikes and jet skis and then you get a chance to see it all again…on screen!

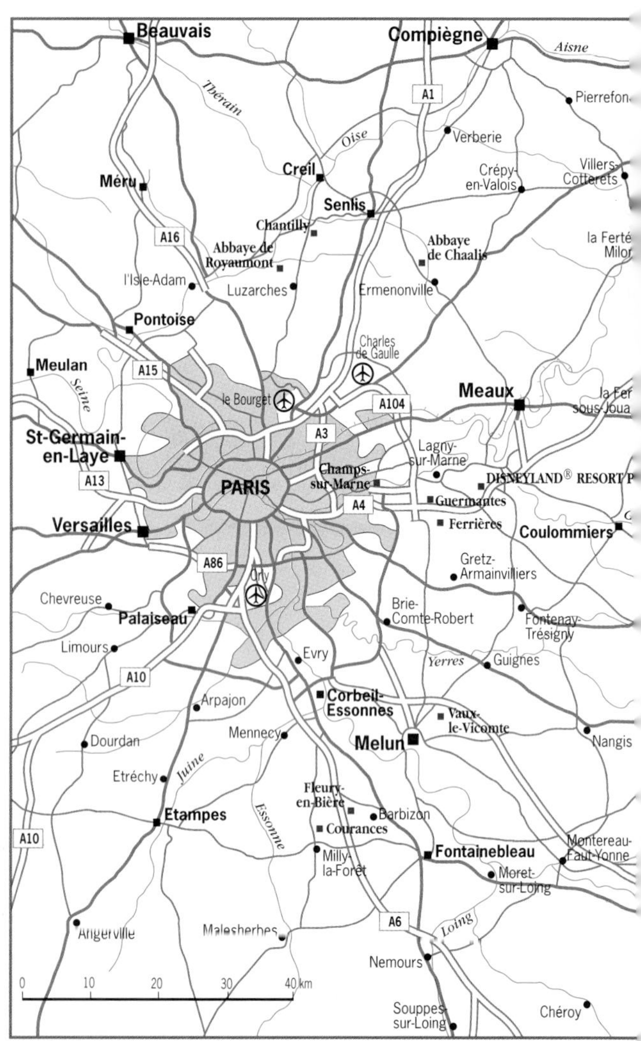

◆

VAL D'EUROPE

10 minutes drive from Disneyland® Resort Paris, exit 13 on the A4 motorway, Val d'Europe station on the A4 RER suburban train from Paris.

A new glass-and-metal complex offering shopping, eating and entertainment on a vast scale has recently sprung up close to Disneyland® Resort

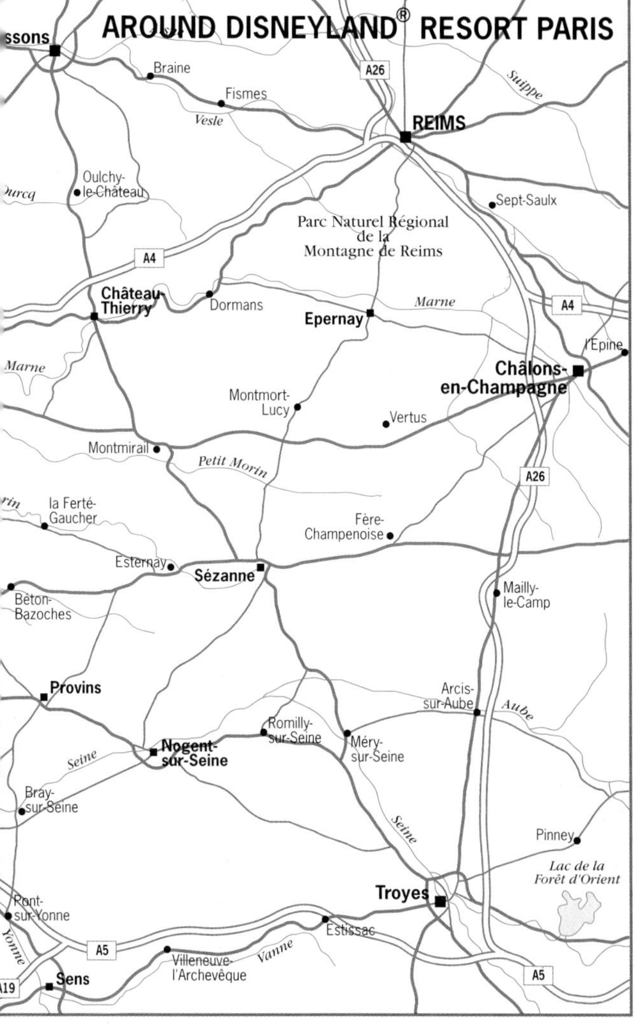

Paris. The International Shopping Centre on two levels includes a hypermarket and over 130 shops as well as **La Vallée Outlet Shopping Village**, a picturesque group of designer boutiques selling previous-season and end-of-line stock at discounted prices. **Les Terrasses** (nine restaurants and two bars) offer a wide choice of menus with live music daily until midnight.

And there is more... **Sealife Val d'Europe** and its 30 aquariums, displaying a fascinating marine world from jellyfish to giant rays and sharks, invite you to journey down the River Seine to the Atlantic and across the ocean to the Caribbean. A fascinating experience as you walk through the 360° underwater glass tunnel. The European Sealife Network presents its own breeding programme for endangered seahorses and its campaign for shark conservation.

Elegant Fontainbleau

HISTORIC CHÂTEAUX

The Île de France, Paris's green belt, is well known for its splendid châteaux and great forests. An hour's drive southwards from Disneyland® Resort Paris will enable you to visit two architectural gems and to explore one of the finest forests in the region.

◆◆◆

Vaux-le-Vicomte, Château de

28 miles (45km) south

Compared with Fontainebleau or Versailles, this château is small, but its moderate size

seems only to enhance its attractiveness and means it can more easily be appreciated and enjoyed in a single visit. The interior contains many charming features and fine antiques, but the grounds are most impressive: illusory vistas, neat topiary, canals and terraced parterres shift before the eye like an Escher painting as you walk among them.
The château has an interesting story. It was built by the ambitious politician Nicolas Fouquet, in 1656: le Vau was the architect, Le Nôtre designed its lovely gardens, and Le Brun supervised the interior. After his gorgeous château was completed in 1661, Fouquet made what was to be a disastrous mistake of inviting Louis XIV to dinner, to impress him. The king was impressed, so impressed that he seethed with jealousy and fury at this parvenu. Fouquet was arrested on a trumped-up charge and his possessions were seized by the king, who commissioned the very same artists to upstage Vaux-le-Vicomte with an even more ambitious project – Versailles. As Fouquet languished in perpetual imprisonment, he must have reflected many times that those who sup with autocratic monarchs need a long spoon.

Fontainebleau

39 miles (63km) south

The massive and beautiful château is the main draw, but the great hunting forest that surrounds the town provides a welcome retreat for Parisians. It is an excellent place for picnics, walking, cycling and riding, but is very busy at weekends. The magnificent royal apartments of the château were transformed from medieval to Renaissance splendour by François I in the 16th century, and later kings also left their mark. The opulence of the decor is astonishing, especially the ceilings.

Stay or Eat:

L'Aigle Noir, 27 place Napoléon Bonaparte (tel: 01 60 74 60 00); there are plenty of less expensive places near the château.

Practical

This section (with the yellow band) includes food, drink, shopping, accommodation, nightlife, tight budget, special events, etc.

FOOD AND DRINK

This is a major element of the entertainment laid on at Disneyland® Resort Paris, and it is a most unusual visitor who leaves without sampling any of it. To do so you would have to provide, carry and store your own supplies, or be prepared to travel some distance to find alternative eating places. There are no food shops or restaurants within walking distance of the resort other than Disney ones, though picnic tables are provided near the Disneyland® Hotel for those who bring their own food. (Remember, you are not allowed to take food or drinks into the Theme Parks.) In any case, eating Disney-style is all part of the experience, and the choice is extensive. Within the Theme Parks there are many different restaurants, serving a great range of ethnic dishes, plus a range of *chariots gourmands* serving speciality foods, such as bagels and stir fry, and a number of carts selling popcorn, ice cream and beverages. In the resort's hotels and campsite there are another dozen or so thematic restaurants (also open to non-hotel residents; it is advisable to make a reservation). At Disney® Village, the entertainment complex just outside the gates of the Disneyland® Resort Paris Theme Parks, there are another half-dozen restaurants, plus a dinner-show venue. Many, but not all the resort's restaurants stay open all day.

Flying high on Dumbo

Whichever Theme Park you are in you will find plenty of places to satisfy any sudden hunger pangs. Some restaurants have table service, at others you queue by counters, and some are no more than take-away snack bars. Child menus or child-size portions are served in table- or counter-service restaurants. Special diets, such as kosher, can also be catered for (with advance warning), as can group meals, birthday treats and business lunches.

At peak times the restaurants within the resort are geared to serve over 150,000 meals. Considering the speed and efficiency with which they do this, the quality is surprisingly high, and at least some notice is taken of many people's wish to eat healthier, less fat-laden diets. Overall, the range of food is very wide, though within each restaurant (particularly the counter-service ones), menu choices are kept reasonably limited for logistical reasons. Inevitably, however, 'fast food' abounds, prepared daily in mass-catering quantities. Where else in France, though, could you dine on a palm-fringed Caribbean shore with boats sliding past your table, or munch spare ribs in a high-raftered Wild West barn full of wagon wheels and hay rakes? Eating at the Disneyland® Resort Paris Theme Parks is not cheap, though some things are good value. If you are on a tight budget, avoid or ration eating at the table-service restaurants. Stick to sensible, filling snacks from the *chariots gourmands*, such as beef and chicken kebabs in Adventureland or baked potatoes in Frontierland. Any of the counter-service restaurants will provide a satisfying plateful of food without breaking the bank if you feel like a sit-down meal, and all table-service restaurants provide a three-course set meal for rather less than the *à la carte* price. You can pay for your meal in cash, and credit cards are accepted (but not by food carts). Guests staying in the resort's hotels may use their Disneyland® Resort Paris charge cards at most places in the Theme Parks (although these are not accepted by food carts either). The amount is then totalled on your credit card bill, which you pay as you check out.

Not Quite Teetotal

Disneyland® Park, like its cousins in Florida, California and Tokyo, was meant to be rigidly alcohol-free. The Theme Parks' priority 'guests' are children, and in such an environment adult pleasures (or vices) were thought to have no place. At first, Walt's strict dictum prevailed even in France, where children grow up accustomed to a watered glass of wine. However, faced with

Tips

- Try to choose off-peak mealtimes to minimise queuing. Eat lunch before midday, or after 2pm, and miss the 8–9pm evening rush if you can. If you have already seen the parades, choose to eat when they are on, as the restaurants are likely to be much emptier.
- At busy holiday times when the Theme Parks are crowded, you can make a same-day-only reservation at any table-service restaurant. The **Blue Lagoon Restaurant** (Adventureland) and **Auberge de Cendrillon** (Fantasyland) usually require booking at peak times. Do not worry if you cannot get into your first choice; there are plenty of other options. The last thing you need worry about here is starving!
- If the Theme Park restaurants seem too busy, simply walk through the gates to Disney® Village, where you will have a choice of another half-dozen eating places, which are probably less busy at lunchtime.

much derision and amazement from the host country the iron Disney rule was eventually bent, just a little, to the satisfaction of most people who did think it slightly odd not to be able to have a glass of wine in a smart, expensive restaurant with an adult atmosphere. Therefore, as a concession to French custom, wine and beer are now served in four of Disneyland® Park's restaurants: **Walt's – an American Restaurant** (Main Street U.S.A.), the **Auberge de Cendrillon** (Fantasyland), the **Blue Lagoon Restaurant** (Adventureland), and the **Silver Spur Steakhouse** (Frontierland). Of course, the Disney® Village restaurants and all the hotels serve alcohol.

All types of ice cream can be enjoyed

Eating in Disneyland® Park

Main Street, U.S.A.

Bagel cart You may spot this in Central Plaza, toasting bagels and adding your choice of toppings. It is just one of many food carts (*chariots gourmands*) selling a variety of snacks and refreshments in the Theme Park.

Cable Car Bake Shop Lots of wicked things most of us should not be eating are on offer in this agreeable (if dark) setting. There is booth seating, decorated with sepia photos of San Franciscan streetcars.

Casey's Corner Head here if you are a baseball freak. Hot dogs and chips are available. Eat them beside bats and balls and Coke logos, and beneath Tiffany lamps. You may be regaled with ragtime music.

The Coffee Grinder The coffee is fresh, but only one kind of coffee (plus espresso) is sold.
Cookie Kitchen A parting-shot temptation as you try to resist the Cable Car Bake Shop. This counter sells muffins and, of course, cookies (biscuits to Europeans).
The Gibson Girl Ice Cream Parlour Milkshakes, sundaes, banana splits and fruity ice-creams are all here in a pink-and-white candy-striped environment, with girls in frilly dresses and straw boaters.
The Ice Cream Company Just that, really.
Market House Deli An old-fashioned general store in the best Disney tradition. Sausages hang from the ceiling, and casks and lovely old tins deck the dresser shelves. There is also an ancient cast-iron stove and an old weighing machine. While admiring the décor, you can munch American sandwiches, such as hot pastrami on rye, and sample turkey and tuna salad.
Plaza Gardens Restaurant A spacious building with an outdoor patio, this is a good place to sit and watch the world, or the parades, go by. The sparkling 19th-century interior is full of columns, statues, stained-glass domes and mirrors. A wide choice of self-service fare consists of salads, hot dishes like Maryland crab cakes, and a luscious array of desserts (included in the price of a main course).
Victoria's Home-Style Cooking Cosy domestic interiors from the 1890s set the

Colonel Hathi's Pizza Outpost serves exotic treats in Adventureland

tone for this counter-service. Eat Victoria's delicious 'pot pies' by the harmonium, or in the conservatory, perhaps watching a passing parade.

Walt's – an American Restaurant One of the smartest restaurants in the Theme Park, this two-storey building offers elegant table service in nine intimate little dining-rooms, all on different themes. Seating inside, or on the outside patio. For good views of the parades, bag an (expensive) table upstairs near the window. Classy American food, including Veal Oscar, rack of lamb with goat's cheese, crab cakes and baked, stuffed Maine lobster. (A cheaper and simpler menu is offered downstairs and on the patio.)

Frontierland

Cowboy Cookout Barbecue A large barn houses this Wild-Western-style barbecue, with inside and outside seating for large numbers. The rustic theme includes agricultural implements, harnesses, quilts, wagon wheels, butter churns and so on, in a hay-loft/grain silo setting.

Fuente del Oro Restaurante Tex-Mex specials are all here: counter-service *tacos* and *fajitas*. The building is an attractive New Mexican one in adobe style, with a courtyard where you can eat and be regaled by the Mariachis, a Mexican group.

Last Chance Café Counter service for sandwiches, turkey drumsticks and beverages. It is carefully styled as a bandit hideout.

The Lucky Nugget Saloon This houses a revue which is shown several times a day and is a counter-service restaurant. The menu features many favourite American dishes.

Silver Spur Steakhouse The smart folks of Thunder Mesa dine here, in stylish 19th-century surroundings, and (needless to say) prime rib steak is the speciality of the house.

Adventureland

Blue Lagoon Restaurant This is located at the entrance of Pirates of the Caribbean, and diners have a view of boats slipping past on their voyage of discovery. The scene – a Caribbean night, lit by torches, with tropical vegetation all around – make this a delightful place to eat. Caribbean specialities and fish predominate: snapper, swordfish and other delicacies wrapped in banana leaves. As it is very popular, it is worth booking in advance if you want a table at a busy time.

Café de la Brousse (summer only) A snack bar with thatched huts on a terrace overlooking Adventure Isle, and a most pleasant place to sit. Sadly, the interesting-sounding North African specialities that were to be sold here have been replaced by hot dogs (albeit spicy ones) and chips, due to the patrons' lack of enthusiasm for anything exotic. Can this really be gastronomic France?

Captain Hook's Galley Sandwiches and cakes are available in this galleon anchored off Skull Rock, which is the haunt of pirates.

Colonel Hathi's Pizza Outpost Tucked away in the bamboo forest, this makes a pleasant retreat. Built in colonial Victorian style, this counter-service restaurant contains mementos of many exciting explorations: native masks, a plane propeller, safari gear, hunting trophies and photographs. You can choose to sit on the veranda, or inside – a central sunken dining area contains a great tropical tree where animated macaws and toucans perch; the Charter Room is a stone-built, cosier room with a fireplace.
Restaurant Agrabah Café Situated at the entrance to Adventureland from Central Plaza, this counter-service restaurant offers a three-course exotic buffet including paella, moussaka, curried lamb, spicy chicken, etc, served with rice and mixed vegetables.
Restaurant Hakuna Matata A counter-service restaurant in an African hut with ethnic animal ceramics, baskets and carvings. Lamb curry and Moroccan meatballs are staples, plus Mickey's fun meal (for children).

Fantasyland
Auberge de Cendrillon Cinderella's country inn is the smartest restaurant in Fantasyland, with beams and a cosy fireplace. You will find Cinderella's pumpkin carriage in an alcove. Hosts and hostesses wear 17th-/18th-century costumes, in keeping with the elegant Louis XIV and XV furnishings. The restaurant serves traditional French cuisine and menus change regularly.

Inside Annette's Diner at Disney® Village

Le Chalet de la Marionnette Fairytale frescos and Tyrolean charm smother this large counter-service restaurant. Chicken and chips and cheeseburgers, followed by apple strudel, are examples of the sort of fare it offers.
Fantasia Gelati Italian ice-creams can be consumed outside on the patio.
March Hare Refreshments A wooden thatched cottage, serving drinks and un-birthday cakes. Bright tables are set outside for the tea party.
The Old Mill This old windmill will make the Dutch feel at home. Snacks, soft drinks and frozen yoghurt are on sale.
Pizzeria Bella Notte Italianate façades set the tone for a feast of pizza and pasta in a setting of hams and garlic. There is also a Bacchic theme of grapes and wine casks.
Toad Hall Restaurant The expansive Mr Toad invites guests to partake of fish and chips wrapped in newspaper and roast beef sandwiches at his fine Elizabethan home. The interior is full of *Wind in the Willows* characters.

Discoveryland
Buzz Lightyear's Pizza Planet Restaurant This pizzeria is conveniently situated close to one of the best attractions in Discoveryland: Honey, I Shrunk the Audience. There is also a children's play area.
Café Hyperion The Jules Verne airship, *Hyperion*, is suspended above the entrance

Colourful signs promise sweet treats

to Videopolis. Inside, this fast counter-service restaurant offers salads, burgers and Italian fast food to carry into the auditorium to sustain you through the show.

Chariots Gourmands A sausage cart (grilled sausages on bread with onions) and a donut cart produce the fastest food in Discoveryland.

Eating in Walt Disney Studios® Park

Restaurant en Coulisse This counter-service restaurant on two floors, with pizzas on the menu, forms part of the glamorous decor of Hollywood Boulevard in Disney Studio 1.

Rendez-vous des Stars Restaurant Undoubtedly the place to be seen! This art-deco-style, buffet-service restaurant serves European cuisine.

Backlot Express Restaurant A counter-service restaurant with a relaxed backstage feel.

Le Café des Cascadeurs Recreating the atmosphere of a studio-staff restaurant during a film shoot

There are also 12 **carts** spread around the park, selling fast food, sandwiches and beverages, which guests can enjoy while sitting at the open **Terrace**.

Eating in Disneyland® Resort Paris Accommodation

Disney's Davy Crockett Ranch® has an attractive log-cabin restaurant, **Crockett's Tavern**, serving American home-style cooking for breakfast (and lunch in peak season) and dinner.

Disneyland® Hotel
California Grill has an elegant open kitchen, where you can see Californian specialities being prepared. **Inventions** specialises in a blow-out buffet at a set price (and also hosts 'Character Breakfasts'). **Café Fantasia** is a pretty, cosy place with many Disney characters incorporated in its décor. This hotel is not the place to enjoy a simple snack at a reasonable price, but worth a try if you can do justice to a full buffet-style breakfast or gourmet dinner.

Disney's Hotel Cheyenne®
Guests eat at the **Chuckwagon Cafe**, a free-flow marketplace along Texan lines, where harnesses and bales of hay deck the high-raftered restaurant.

Disney's Hotel New York®
Its restaurants are slick and smart, redolent of cocktails and dinner-dances and Big Band music. **Manhattan Restaurant** offers a 1930s experience reminiscent of Harlem's 'Cotton Club', with fine dining in luxurious surroundings. The **Manhattan Lounge** is the perfect venue for aperitifs or after-dinner drinks, while the **Parkside Diner** is also a good place to enjoy an evening drink or a casual (but chic) meal.

Disney's Hotel Santa Fe®
La Cantina is an imaginative Tex-Mex desert café, with petrol pumps and pick-up trucks among the food-stalls (an excellent place for breakfast).

Disney's Newport Bay Club®
The **Yacht Club** is a speciality seafood restaurant, and from the **Cape Cod** restaurant guests overlook a flashing lighthouse by the shores of Lake Disney®, where 'Toobie' boats bob in summer.

Disney's Sequoia Lodge®
Hearty grills and spit-roasts are available in the **Hunter's Grill**, while **The Beaver Creek Tavern** is a good place for relaxing family meals. **Redwood Bar and Lounge** has a warm atmosphere.

Eating in Disney® Village
Several types of American food can be eaten at the ten restaurants and snack bars.
Annette's Diner This is a 50s-style restaurant serving burgers and milkshakes amid period music (Elvis, Chuck Berry), while waitresses on roller skates dash up and down.
Billy Bob's Country Western Saloon This Nashville saloon resounds with country-and-western music. Enjoy a fixed-price Texas-style buffet with wine or beer.
Buffalo Bill's Wild West Show (See **Nightlife and Entertainment**, page 99).
Café Mickey Overlooking Lake Disney®, this two-storey restaurant and cocktail bar offers Californian specialities and a good selection of wines.
McDonald's The fast food offers no surprises but the Commedia dell'Arte decor is original, and there is a large play area based on the theme of Leonardo da Vinci's discoveries.

Dance all evening at Billy Bob's Country Western Saloon

Planet Hollywood® This spherical restaurant at the entrance of Disney® Village serves Californian cuisine in a movie decor.
Rainforest Café The building looks like a mud hut, an appropriate style for the equatorial rainforest, and the restaurant is dedicated to the protection of animals.
New York Style Sandwiches A New York deli, where giant pickle jars and elaborate speciality bread form the window display. Hot pastrami on rye, cream cheese on a bagel, or a classic bologna could precede Manhattan spice cake. You get substantial side dishes of potato salad or coleslaw.
Sports Bar Provides a non-stop round of televised sport on numerous TV monitors. TV dinners take the form of hot dogs and sandwiches.
The Steakhouse Prime rib and T-bones are served in a building evoking a Chicago meat-packing warehouse. Classic wines (many Californian), and good desserts, such as brownies and cheesecakes, are sold.

SHOPPING

'Merchandising' is all part of the entertainment at Disneyland® Resort Paris, and you will find shops everywhere: in the hotels, at Disney® Village, and throughout both of the Theme Parks. It is obviously a highly profitable operation for the Disney organisation, and the commercial tone may displease some visitors. But how much time and money you want to spend shopping is entirely up to you. Just look if you like, and

Mickey Mouse appears on much Disney merchandise

move on. It is a rare child, however, who will not take home at least one reminder of a trip to the resort. Souvenirs come in all price ranges, from sweets at a few cents to a beautiful glass model of Cinderella's coach at €12,000. Prices of goods at Disneyland® Resort Paris are not low, but then neither is quality, even in items that are mass-produced and basically ephemeral. Whatever you feel about the aesthetics of mouse ears, at least they are not likely to disintegrate the second you walk out of the shop. Disney's rigorous standards apply to every item sold on its property, and that amounts to over 22,000 different pieces of merchandise in more than 40 shops. The shops here are just as much an attraction as the rides.

Shops in Disneyland® Park

Main Street, U.S.A.

Bixby Brothers Men's Accessories Situated on Town Square, this elegant shop sells watches, ties, caps, hats, fancy socks and underwear for the man about town.

Boardwalk Candy Palace No children (and very few adults) get past this in a hurry. Here there are sweets and fudge, chocolates and toffees of all shapes and hues. Glass pillars, jars and a Ferris Wheel are filled with a kaleidoscopic range. Almost behind the scenes, the fudge-makers are hard at work. You can also buy saltwater taffy.

Crystal Art Yet more Disney souvenirs, in a yesteryear fairground setting. Mickey and Minnie wave from a hot-air balloon. Watch the man making cute little animals out of molten glass at Glass Fantasies.

Dapper Dan's Hair Cuts A splendid old-style barber's shop with a striped pole outside; inside among the tiles, mahogany and marble are badger-hair brushes and personal shaving mugs. You can have a haircut for about €18, or a haircut and old-fashioned shave for €30.

Disney Clothiers, Ltd Fashion gear in a draper's shop, set in a private house of the period.

Disney & Co Children's clothing, toys and gifts.

Disneyana Collectibles Ceramics, jewellery boxes, lithographs, and the inked 'cels' from Disney animation pictures.

Emporium Mostly devoted to Disney souvenirs, this is the largest store in the Theme Park. The old-fashioned pneumatic overhead cash transport system is fun to watch.

Harrington's Fine China & Porcelains The interior of crystal, stained glass and *faux* marble sets off a glittering array of glass and china. Some hand-painting takes place here.

Lilly's Boutique sells tableware, crystal items, bathrobes and towels, perfumed soap, hand towels decorated with Disney characters.

Main Street Motors (see page 40)

Plaza Est and **Plaza West Boutiques** Two stands on Central Plaza selling Disney souvenirs and gifts.

Ribbons & Bows Hat Shop
Also on Town Square, this shop sells Victorian-style millinery and lots of other things to stick on your head, including hair slides, combs and mouse ears. You can also have a monogram embroidered for free by an old-fashioned sewing machine.
Silhouette Artist If you fancy your profile sketched, you've come to the right place!
The Storybook Store On Town Square. Disney film classics are retold in many languages – *Peter Pan*, *Alice in Wonderland* and so on. Also available are cassettes, novelty stationery, and Tigger is waiting to stamp your books with a Disneyland® Park memento.

Town Square Photography
Film, video cassettes and other photographic equipment is sold here, in a setting of aged camera gear. There are also repair and express developing services, and cameras and video cameras for hire.

Frontierland
Pueblo Trading Post
Interesting range of ethnic Mexican and Indian crafts: rugs, pottery, jewellery, dolls, etc.
Thunder Mesa Mercantile Building A vast array of Wild West accoutrements, including jeans, coonskin caps, stetsons, cowboy boots and so on, is

The Emporium in Main Street

available at this log cabin. Also Wild-Western-style provisions.

Adventureland

Situated on either side of the entrance to Adventureland are **Les Trésors de Schéhérazade** offering sandalwood boxes, brass bells and perfume bottles, and **La Girafe Curieuse** selling an array of safari clothing and accessories.

Le Coffre du Capitaine Pirate gear is on sale in this shop at the exit of Pirates of the Caribbean: pieces-of-eight, cutlasses, eye-patches, skull-and-crossbone hats and flags.

Indiana Jones™ Adventure Outpost A tantalising collection of odd souvenirs from interesting parts of the globe: jewellery, shells and the necessities of exploration, such as a watch incorporating a compass.

Fantasyland

Geppetto's Workshop
More unusual toys: music boxes, cuckoo clocks, puzzles, marionettes and baby clothes.

La Boutique du Château
Within the castle, this festive shop is a year-round hoard of Christmas decorations.

La Chaumière des Sept Nains
More Disney apparel and stuffed toys, in the cottage of the Seven Dwarfs.

La Confiserie des Trois Fées
Edible goodies in the forest cottage of three good fairies from *Sleeping Beauty*.

Merlin l'Enchanteur Within the castle, this shop is hard to resist. Designed as the magician's workshop, the walls are full of intriguing inventions and glittering toys: figurines, kaleidoscopes, chess sets and even a jewelled crown. Everything your child needs to become a real magician and the costume that goes with it.

Sir Mickey's Mickey Mouse is shown fighting with a giant beanstalk here.

Discoveryland

Constellations Souvenirs for explorers, hi-tech toys and Disney clothes in a startling room rather like a planetarium. An alchemist's still and other scientific instruments decorate the shop. Leonardo's *Ornithopter* flying machine hangs from the ceiling, with Mickey Mouse at the controls.

The Disney Store in Disney® Village

Star Traders All kinds of space-age gadgets and games can be found in this octagonal building: hologram badges, puzzles, etc.

Shops in Walt Disney Studios® Park

Front Lot

Walt Disney Studios Store, the largest boutique in the Park, offers a variety of toys, clothes and souvenirs, as well as a photo development service.
Studio Photo inside the Studio Services precinct, sells cameras, films and souvenirs.
Legends of Hollywood Striking decors straight out of a movie with an array of souvenirs and gifts from beach gear to toy cars.

Animation Courtyard

The Disney Animation Gallery displays a variety of Disney collectibles.

Backlot

Rock Around the Shop, at the exit of the Rock'n'Roller Coaster ride, is packed with a choice of music-themed souvenirs.

Shops in Disneyland® Resort Paris

The Hotels

Each of the hotel shops, besides stocking a range of staples, features a few special items appropriate to its theme. So Disney's Hotel Cheyenne's® shop sells Wild West gear, and Disney's Hotel Santa Fe's® shop stocks cactus mugs. Do not bother to shop around within the resort; prices are identical for the same items everywhere. Images of Mickey Mouse are endlessly reproduced on all manner of artefacts: soft toys, mugs, pencils, T-shirts, sweets and novelties of all kinds. All the hotel shops have significant store space for Disney goods. The **Post Office** is in Marne-la-Vallée Station but stamps can also be bought at hotels.

Disney® Village

The Disney Store has a collection of transport – trains, planes, cars – amid a vast range of 'character merchandise' and clothes for the whole family. The **Disney Gallery** offers high-quality plates and objects. **Team Mickey** sells Mickey Mouse sportswear, and **Hollywood Pictures** has movie souvenirs (posters, books, photographs and so on), many from The Walt Disney Studios® Park, whereas **Planet Hollywood Boutique** sells themed clothes and accessories. More out of the ordinary is Disney® Village's **Buffalo Trading Company** and the **Rainforest Café Boutique**. Children will be fascinated by the **World of Toys**.

Tips

- Beware of spending too much time in the shops. You will regret not going on the rides if you run out of time, and there are plenty of shops outside the Theme Park to browse in at leisure.
- If you want to do some shopping, do not leave things to the last minute, when queues are long. Shop in the early or mid-afternoon, when you feel like a break. You can always leave bulky things in the lockers beneath Main Street Station, or leave your purchases at the shop and then pick them up from 5pm at Town Square Terrace.
- The 'user-friendly' Disney shops may seem a klepto-maniac's paradise. Security is very, very low key, but it certainly exists and 'appropriate measures' are taken if necessary.
- Besides cash (euros), you can pay for items in Disney stores by traveller's cheque, Eurocheque or credit card (American Express, Visa, Diner's Club or Eurocard/Mastercard only). Personal cheques may only be drawn on French banks, and you will need ID. If you are staying in one of the resort's hotels, you can use your Disney card to charge purchases directly to your credit card account. Currency exchange offices are also available at City Hall, in Adventureland (seasonal) and Fantasyland.
- If by any chance something you buy is faulty, take it back to the shop with your receipt and it will be exchanged. If you have left the Theme Park, send the item, with a photocopy of the receipt and a letter explaining the defect to the manager of the store where you bought it. Write to him or her c/o Merchandising Department, Disneyland® Paris, BP 100, F-77777 Marne-la-Vallée, CEDEX 4, France. You will then receive a refund or exchange of purchase.

ACCOMMODATION

Visitors can choose to stay at one of the seven Disneyland® Resort Paris themed hotels. You will then be able to enjoy certain privileges denied to off-site visitors, such as guaranteed access to the Theme Parks (which may close to other visitors on severely crowded days). The hotels themselves are imaginatively designed and very comfortable, each a separate mini-theme park in itself – Manhattan or New Mexican, New English or Wild Western. If you want a total Disney experience, you should stay at the resort. All the hotels (apart from Disney's Davy Crockett Ranch®) are within walking distance of the entrance gates to the Disneyland® Resort Paris Theme Parks, though to make life even easier a fleet of buses whirls round the resort at frequent intervals, taking visitors to the bus station, less than five minutes' walk from the turnstiles. Although the Disney's Davy Crockett Ranch® is several kilometres away, it is assumed that visitors have a car and free parking is available to them close to the Theme Parks.

You can choose to stay at a hotel or motel outside the resort, but none are within walking distance. If you have notions of staying in some quaint country *auberge* within a few minutes' drive of the resort, dispel them now. Most accommodation that serves the Disneyland® Resort Paris area of Marne-la-Vallée is modern and purely functional, consisting of box-like motels or business hotels.

If you are touring the area by car, and fancy a day or two at Disneyland® Resort Paris (but do not regard the Disney experience as of paramount importance), you might choose to stay further afield in a place of historic interest, such as Meaux or Fontainebleau, or even perhaps in the Champagne country to the east. You should be prepared for a drive of an hour or more to reach the resort.

Last but not least, you can opt to stay in Paris and travel each day to Disneyland® Resort Paris by public transport. Many tour operators also offer inclusive deals using French or Disneyland® Resort Paris hotels at all price levels.

Disneyland® Resort Paris Hotels

Three hotels under construction at Disneyland Resort Paris will increase room capacity by 1,100 from spring 2003 onwards. The seven existing hotels all lie quite close together just outside the gates of the Theme Parks, around the artificial stretches of water christened **Lake Disney®** and **Rio Grande**. Hotels are classified in three categories: two, three or four stars. The more expensive ones are closer to the Theme Parks entrance gates. Each hotel is very different in appearance, but all are highly theatrical, endeavouring to give their guests a variety of thematic experiences, as each one embodies in a vivid way a universally recognisable aspect of the USA, either past or

Disneyland® Hotel

present – from the sophistication of Manhattan to the seclusion of the national parks, the pioneer spirit of the Wild West and the lazy southern atmosphere of a New Mexico village. The hotel architecture is a subject in itself. Several world-renowned architects have created the hotels, and the ways in which themes have been encapsulated are startling and innovative.

All of the resort hotels have high standards of comfort and cleanliness, and aim to provide the level of service appropriate to any Disney facility. When the resort first opened, however, staffing levels seemed inadequate to cope with queues at reception areas, and some waiting times were unacceptably long. The more expensive hotels have more elaborate trappings than the economy ones, but all of them have some non-smoking rooms, and some are suitable for the disabled. All except Disney's Hotel Santa Fe® and Disney's Hotel Cheyenne® have swimming pools and health clubs. Note that there is no porter service at the two-star hotels, or at the campsite, so travel light! These complexes are large and spread out.

Hotels are open all year round but hotel rates fluctuate according to season, so check all reservation details first with your travel agent or with Disneyland® Resort Paris Reservations (see the **Directory** on page 121 for telephone numbers and Internet address).

Disneyland® Hotel

(Four-star – 496 rooms)

This rambling pink confection is one of the most striking land-marks of Disneyland® Resort Paris. In terms of bedrooms it is the smallest of the hotels, though you would never think so to look at it. Its florid, Victorian-style gables and turrets, topped with pointed white finials, triumphantly straddle the entrance gates to

Newport Bay Club®

Disneyland® Park. From Main Street, just inside the turnstiles, it is as noticeable a fantasy feature as the castle, and many rooms have views of the Theme Park. The hotel seems utterly confident of its status as the flagship, and it is easily the most Disneyesque of all the strange buildings in the resort area. Designed by the architects of Disney 'Imagineering', it evokes the grand seaside palaces that graced the smart resorts of Florida and California at the turn of the 20th century. It is very much a family hotel, with thematic references to Disney cartoon characters. A giant Mickey Mouse clock on the central façade shows guests the time. The hotel's main features are a huge reception lobby, whose chandelier drips with ivy leaves, and a promenade, where a piano is played in an elegant lounge. The two restaurants and themed café offer a variety of lavish fare. This is the most expensive hotel in the resort, with many luxury facilities. Finding your way around its complex blocks, though, takes some time. The hotel also offers Castle Club VIP service with luxurious suites, a private lounge, where breakfast is available and soft drinks are served all day, and additional privileges for an extra charge (including direct access to the Theme Park).

Disney's Hotel New York®
(Four-star – 563 rooms)
If you have seen Florida's Walt Disney World Resort you will instantly recognise the post-modernist handiwork of the celebrated American architect Michael Graves. His fantasy hotels in Orlando have a similarly extravagant style. Disney's Hotel New York® recreates the landscapes of the Big Apple (minus those unforgettable exterior fire escapes) in a subtle palette of warm terracotta, dove grey and soft salmon. Inside, every last feature of the hotel, down to the Empire State Building lampstands in the bedrooms, echoes the theme. The effect is sophisticated, but fun. It is a more adult environment than the Disneyland® Hotel, and this hotel hosts Disney's lucrative sideline, the convention business (a very large conference centre is attached, providing some of the most extensive meeting-room

facilities in the Paris area). Rooms overlook paved plazas or shady gardens and tennis courts. Though it's in the same category, Disney's Hotel New York® is slightly less expensive than the Disneyland® Hotel.

Disney's Newport Bay Club®
(Three-star – 1,093 rooms)
The irregular, creamy clapboard architecture with the grey-green roofs conjures up a tang of salt spray and a whiff of ozone. This is New England, the Atlantic seaboard. The New York architect Robert Stern designed this elaborate whimsy with classical touches, reminiscent of the Yacht and Beach Clubs at Walt Disney World Resort in Florida. Inside, the atmosphere is elegantly restful in shades of blue and grey. Bedrooms and corridors continue the nautical theme, with porthole windows and ship's tiller headboards. The **Fisherman's Wharf** bar-lounge is relaxing to sit in. The hotel has its own convention centre.

Disney's Sequoia Lodge®
(Three-star – 1,011 rooms)
Embryonic redwood forests surround the timber wings and shallow, copper-green rooftops of this hotel, bent on recreating the atmosphere of an American National Park lodge. Décor consists of lots of redwood veneer and grey stone. The main feature of the bar area is a huge, stone-faced fireplace, where there are real log fires. The imaginative swimming pool has waterslides and hot springs, and is one of this hotel's most attractive points. Bedrooms are decorated with wooden furniture and patchwork quilts.

Disney's Hotel Cheyenne®
(Two-star – 1,000 rooms)
A taste of the Old Wild West. Here you will find a life-size stage set of *High Noon*, where covered wagons stand in the streets, and you check in at the Town Bank by the Hangman's Tree. You could be sleeping in any one of 14 separate, wood-framed buildings. The **Red Garter Saloon** is the place for a drink, but do not expect a peaceful time here. It is very much geared to families, and the atmosphere is cheerfully gregarious. In the bedrooms, Western fans will be delighted to find stetson hat mirrors and bucking broncos on the walls, while **Fort Apache**, in the grounds, is a new style of adventure playground.

Disney's Hotel Santa Fe®
(Two-star – 1,000 rooms)
We are somewhere in New Mexico at this hotel, marked by a large 'drive-in cinema screen' sign bearing the likeness of Clint Eastwood. A complex of blocks encapsulating the atmosphere of the desert lies behind it, with colours ranging from blues and violets to earth tones. Between the blocks are mysterious sculpted objects, a flying saucer, a volcano, rusting automobiles and giant cacti. The theories behind the architecture of this hotel are complex, and it is worth following the various 'trails' between the buildings that architect Antoine Predock created (the Trail of Legends, the Trail of Infinite Space, and

so on). Bedrooms are tastefully designed, using Pueblo Indian themes. Of the two economy hotels, Disney's Hotel Santa Fe® costs slightly less.

Disney's Davy Crockett Ranch®

(498 cabins, 97 campsites)
The campsite is some way from the Theme Parks, south of the A4 beyond the golf course, so be prepared to use your car on a regular basis since there is no bus service available.
However, parking near the Theme Parks is free to guests of Disney's Davy Crockett Ranch®. An extensive 140-acre (57ha) patch of mature oak and beech woodland allows visitors to sample an outdoor experience in pioneer style. By staying in one of the luxurious trailer-home cabins, you can do so in great comfort. There is a microwave oven, telephone, toaster, dishwasher, maid service (every other day), and a large colour TV. Breakfast is included and can be eaten in Crockett's Tavern or collected and taken back to your cabin. If you prefer, you can bring your own tent or caravan and set up camp in the trees, cooking baked beans over a primus stove or taking advantage of Crockett's Tavern. Each site is supplied with water, toilets and electricity, as well as a barbecue and picnic table. Other features include a small farm of domestic animals, sports facilities (tennis, volleyball, basketball, *pétanque*), and a beautiful and cleverly landscaped swimming pool with waterfalls, bridges, whirlpools, slides and water cannon, housed in a huge, light and airy log cabin. Bicycles or electric golf carts can be hired to ride round the site. An on-site shop provides a wide range of groceries and toiletries, films, sweets and toys.

Off-site Accommodation

Numerous box-like motels are springing up around Marne-la-Vallée to cater for the new influx of visitors. Many of these belong to chains such as Campanile, Primevère, Mercure, Altea, Fimotel, Climat, Ibis, Novotel or Formule 1, providing 1- to 3-star accommodation. Do not expect anything very fancy or interesting; these are purely intended to provide practical, adequate accommodation for brief stop-overs. Many are in charmless locations on busy roads and suffer from traffic noise; a few are handily placed for the RER stations on the Marne-la-Vallée line, but you generally need a car. Most provide some sort of restaurant, where the food, if not exactly *haute cuisine*, is authentically French and less expensive than in Disneyland® Resort Paris. Many establishments work with tour operators, and you will find them listed in brochures offering Disneyland® Resort Paris packages. Most of the big chains produce brochures, with useful location plans. If you prefer small, privately run family hotels, get the local *Logis de France* list. The Île-de-France Maison du Tourisme (opposite Disney® Village) produces a useful list of local accommodation

Meeting Mickey at a character breakfast in Disneyland® Hotel

and is very helpful about where to stay. It will make reservations for a small fee.

Suggested Off-Site Hotels
Three good, newish hotels near Disneyland® Paris Resort are modelled closely on American motel chains: the **Novotel Marne-la-Vallée**, Collégien (tel: 01 64 80 53 53), the **Golf Hôtel** at 15 avenue du Golf, Bussy-St-Georges (tel: 01 64 66 30 30), and the **Hôtel du Moulin de Paris**, Magny-le-Hongre (tel: 01 60 43 77 77). The latest arrival on the scene and the closest to Disneyland® Resort Paris is the three-star **Hôtel l'Élysée Val d'Europe** (located at the Val d'Europe International Shopping Centre, just a five-minute RER ride from the Disney Theme Parks). Less expensive, independent small hotels with slightly more character include **Acostel**, 336 avenue de la Victoire (R.N.3), Meaux (tel: 01 64 33 28 58); **Demeure de la Catounière**, 1 rue de l'Église, Sancy-les-Meaux (tel: 01 60 25 71 74); and **Auberge du Cheval Blanc**, 2 rue de Lagny, Jossigny (tel: 01 64 02 24 27). If you like a more expensive and luxurious place, with peaceful settings and more ambitious facilities, slightly further from the resort, then the **Auberge de Gonfalon**, 2 rue de l'Église, Germiny l'Évêque (tel: 01 64 33 16 05), a quiet, stylish hotel by the River Marne is exactly what you are looking for.

Staying Further Afield
The countryside immediately around Disneyland® Resort Paris is of little interest, but Fontainebleau, within one hour's drive, has good hotels, and is well worth a visit. (See **Excursions from Disneyland® Resort Paris** on pages 72–5) .

Staying in Paris
There is little point in choosing to stay in one of Paris's non-descript easterly suburbs,

thinking you will be that much nearer the Theme Parks. You will miss out on both the bright lights of Disneyland® Resort Paris and the bright lights of Paris. You may not even save travelling time; many RER trains skip stations between Vincennes and Marne-la-Vallée, so the service from outer suburbs can be less frequent than from the centre. There is obviously a vast number of hotels to choose from in Paris, and you will see these listed in tour operators' brochures at all price levels and in all areas. If you are booking independently, one of the best areas to choose is the Marais district (postcode 75004) where the Pompidou Centre and Hôtel de Ville lie north of Notre-Dame. There are three reasons for this: first, it is one of the most interesting and charming areas of old Paris; second, it has a number of small, good-value hotels of real character; and third, it is on RER line A4 to Disneyland® Resort Paris, taking about 40 minutes from Châtelet–les–Halles or the Gare de Lyon (see the **Directory** on pages 113–14, for more about transport).

Disneyland® Park excels at parades

Suggested Parisian Hotels
Hôtel Caron de Beaumarchais, 12 rue Vieille-du-Temple (tel: 01 42 72 34 12); **Hôtel de la Bretonnerie**, 22 rue Ste-Croix-de-la-Bretonnerie (tel: 01 48 87 77 63); **Hôtel St Merry**, 78 rue de la Verrerie (tel: 01 42 78 14 15); **Hôtel du Vieux Marais**, 8 rue du Plâtre (tel: 01 42 78 47 22); **Hôtel de la Place des Vosges**, 12 rue de Birague (tel: 01 42 72 60 46); **Hôtel Axial Beaubourg**, 11 rue du Temple (tel: 01 42 72 72 22); **Hôtel St Louis**, 75 rue St-Louis-en-l'Ile (tel: 01 46 34 04 80).

Packages
The standard price of a basic Disneyland® Resort Paris package (including two nights, breakfast and three days' unlimited Theme Park access) ranges from about £106 to nearly £200 per person in high season (2002 rates), though it is worth remembering that most resort hotel bedrooms take four people. However, inclusive Disneyland® Resort Paris packages offer one extra night in the same hotel and one extra day in the Disney Theme Parks if you book and pay for a three-night 'Classic' package through Disney's Central Reservation Office. If you book a package at a resort hotel, or at Disney's Davy Crockett Ranch® (cabins only, not tents), you get unlimited entry to the Theme Park during your stay, as well as use of local transport, welcome cocktails and so on (you make your own way to Disneyland® Resort Paris). Contact Disneyland® Resort Paris Central Reservations on 08705 03 03 03 (national rate call), for

further details, including the Disneyland® Resort Paris brochure, Disneyland® Resort Paris Official Guide (brochure). (See also page 121.)

Many tour operators offer package deals which include travel to the resort and Theme Parks entrance fees. You stay either at Disneyland® Resort Paris hotels, or at off-site motels nearby, or at hotels in Paris. What you buy with a package holiday is the convenience of having all arrangements made for you, by agents with more influence than an independent traveller. If you decide to book a package holiday, look first at Disneyland® Resort Paris 'preferred travel partners' (including Air France, P&O Stena Line, Eurotunnel, Eurostar), and at the resort's 'selected operators': Paris Travel Service, Cresta Holidays, Leger Coach Tours, Bridge Travel Service, Sovereign Holidays, Thomas Cook Holidays and Thompson Breakaway. All these operators offer package holidays at Disneyland® Resort Paris hotels and have a privileged relationship with the Disney organisation, entitling clients to certain priority treatment. Prices, even among these operators, vary widely for substantially the same package. A great many other operators offer packages, many of them using much cheaper accommodation off site. Take care to read the small print about what your package actually includes and how much time you will have at the Theme Parks. Beware of some cheap coach tours that exclude Theme Parks admission costs, or the cost of transfer to hotels.

NIGHTLIFE AND ENTERTAINMENT

While the Theme Parks are open Disneyland® Resort Paris is one long round of entertainment. Besides all the individual attractions, there is always something extra going on somewhere. As you arrive in Disneyland® Park you are greeted by smartly dressed marching bands or instrumentalists. In the different lands of the Theme Park, you will find other musicians: an African steel band here, or a Mexican group there. Impromptu scenes may surprise you: for instance, a sudden shoot-out on the rooftops of **The Lucky Nugget Saloon**. In Frontierland you may encounter the **card-sharp** doing his version of Find the Lady (he is not allowed to take money from anyone). Not all these entertainers are in Disneyland® Park every day. Ask at **City Hall** if you want to see anything in particular.

Within Walt Disney Studios® Park, back-to-back performances by actors, musicians and characters help to set the scene of a real working film studio. Ask at Studio Services for details of where to catch the acts.

Regular Shows in Disneyland® Park

Performances take place several times a day, at **Le Théâtre du Château**, **Videopolis**, **Fantasy Festival**

Buffalo Bill's Wild West Show

Stage or the **Chaparral Theatre** (featuring the Tarzan Encounter May–Sep). As you go into the Theme Park, be sure to pick up an *Entertainment Program* listing show times. The programme rotates weekly, and most shows last about 20 minutes. The **Fantasy Festival Stage** hosts performances of music and dancing as well as special events such as Christmas shows. **Mulan, the Legend**, an acrobatic musical show staged four times a day in the Videopolis auditorium, with 32 Chinese acrobats joining the main *Mulan* characters.

Parades and Fireworks

For full details of these, refer to the **What to See** pages 38–9.

Dinner Shows

At present there are two dinner shows, one in Disneyland® Park's Frontierland (at **The Lucky Nugget Saloon**), the other at **Disney® Village**. **The Lucky Nugget Saloon**, all gilded lights and tasselled curtains, is horseshoe-shaped like a theatre, and puts on several 30-minute shows a day. The plot is a corny but enjoyable tale of a fun-loving gal who strikes it rich and heads for Paris, where she encounters Pierre Paradis, the man of her dreams, and collects a dance troupe. **Buffalo Bill's Wild West Show** is more expensive, involving stunt riding, lasso tricks and some bewildered buffalo. It is an enthusiastically presented show featuring 'Annie Oakley' (best of the riders), and assorted cowboys and Indians. Based on the touring Wild West Show which wowed France in the 1889 Exposition Universelle, the theme continues to fascinate its European audience. Western-style spare ribs and chilli accompany the show. There is plenty of opportunity for audience participation

Disney® Village

When the Theme Parks close, there are still things to do. In Disney® Village there is a nightclub and bars, shops and restaurants that all stay open late, as well as multi-screen cinemas (including one with a giant screen). **Hurricanes** is the venue for dancing, with 'high-energy' lighting and music, and sunset parties on the veranda (free admission for Disney Hotel guests). **Billy Bob's Country Western Saloon** has Western music and a Texan atmosphere. **Rock 'n' Roll America** is a bar serving drinks and pizzas to the sounds of live rock and roll bands. In addition, various live concerts take place on certain dates throughout the year.

Hotel Entertainment
Following the development of night entertainment in Disney® Village, only a stone's throw from most hotels, hotel entertainment is very low-key these days. However, **Disney's Davy Crockett Ranch®** and, to a lesser extent, **Disney's Hotel Cheyenne®** continue to provide live country music and karaoke evenings on a regular basis.

Outside Disneyland® Resort Paris
Among the bright lights of Paris any number of high- or low-brow entertainments or restaurants await visitors, from the fleshpots of Pigalle and the Moulin Rouge to the Opéra, or Left-Bank café-théâtre. The tourist office outside Marne-la-Vallée will give you lots of advice. Get one of the 'What's On' magazines, such as *L'Officiel des Spectacles* or *Pariscope* (out each Wednesday) for full listings. On Thursdays the Musée d'Orsay, one of Paris's most enjoyable museums, stays open late; and on Mondays or Wednesdays you can visit sections of the Louvre until 10pm. After dark, Paris looks stunning from the top of the Eiffel Tower (open till 11pm), and the Bateaux Mouches run during the evenings, too. Remember to check the time of your last train (usually at about 12.30am) back to Marne-la-Vallée!
In an attempt not to be outshone in the contest for tourist revenue are several historic towns near Disneyland® Resort Paris. They put on *son et lumière* shows and other events during the summer (Meaux, Fontainebleau and Chantilly). And you can also visit Vaux-le-Vicomte by candlelight on some summer Saturdays.

Main Street, U.S.A. is just as lively once the sun has set

SPECIAL EVENTS

Besides the big parades that take place daily, or whenever Disneyland® Park is open late, special holidays are marked by extra-spectacular extravaganzas. New Year, for example, witnesses even more fireworks than usual and parties in all the hotels. Special parades are held periodically throughout the year. Needless to say, Christmas is celebrated with carols and a tree. Other events are planned at shorter notice during the year.

If you are thinking of combining a visit to Disneyland® Resort Paris with other major events, you will find Paris an ideal centre (apart from during August, when many Parisians leave the city for their holidays). In Paris, fashion shows start in January. They are followed by the Paris Fair in April; the biennial Paris Air Show and Paris Festival in May; French Open tennis championships in June, and special events to mark Bastille Day on 14 July. There are also the final stages of the Tour de France bicycle race to enjoy. During the autumn there are exhibitions, concerts and the like. A free brochure called *Fêtes et Manifestations*, listing major exhibitions and events in Paris and Île-de-France, is available at the French Tourist Office, 127 avenue des Champs-Élysées, 75009 Paris (tel. 08 36 68 31 12). If any of these events coincide with your stay, book non-Disneyland® Resort Paris accommodation well in advance to avoid disappointment. Several other places within easy reach of Disneyland® Resort Paris have special events, too. In Meaux, for example, there is a summer festival with *son et lumière* in the

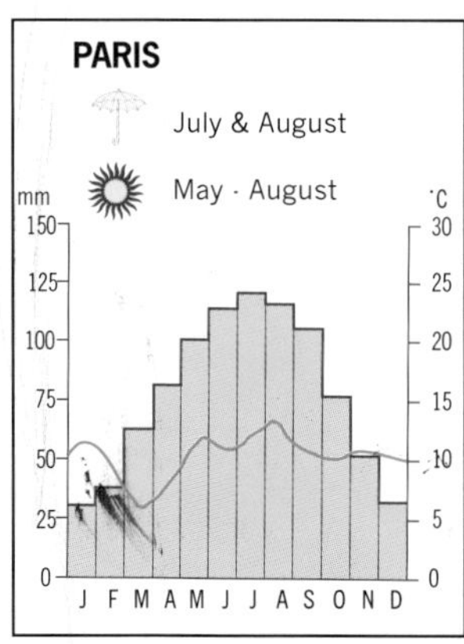

The Cheshire Cat points the way in Alice's Curious Labyrinth

grounds of the Bishop's Palace. Reims, too, has its viticultural calendar when champagne grapes are harvested. At Fontainebleau surprised visitors may discover a party of *belle époque* Parisians in splendid costumes strolling through the gardens, while Vaux-le-Vicomte offers tours by candlelight on some Saturday nights. The **tourist office** outside Marne-la-Vallée Station can provide details.

THE WEATHER AND WHEN TO GO

When Disneyland® Park was first planned, there was some debate over Disney's prudence in placing it in cool Northern France, instead of in Spain or somewhere near the Mediterranean. There is no doubt that climate will play a significant role in the future success of Disneyland® Resort Paris, perhaps more than anyone would have imagined. Keen Disney fans who remember the sunshine of Florida or California may be dismayed to find chilly European drizzle and cloud. The facts are incontrovertible: the resort looks truly magical in the sun, when its colours sparkle and the gilded finials of the castle glitter. On dull days it is just not the same. If you have any choice in the matter, try to visit on a fine day. But do not abandon the idea of going simply because the weather is poor. For one thing, the Theme Parks are almost certain to be less crowded, and you will see far more attractions. Disney 'Imagineers' have considered the weather, of course, and have made a number of modifications to the design of the Theme Parks to suit Northern France's climate. All visitor areas have central heating and air conditioning, and in many places, particularly in hotels, shops and restaurants, you will find cheerful log fires roaring away. More of the attractions and queuing areas are covered over than in Disney Theme Parks in America, and most hotel swimming pools are covered. Large eaves also extend over queuing areas to protect waiting crowds at the attractions.

Marne-la-Vallée's climate, described as 'temperate' in Disney's promotional literature, is actually rather dryer than that of coastal France. The wettest months are from November to January and from March to May (all have more than 15 days of rainfall – not necessarily, of course, all day long). Highest temperatures are predictably in July and August, when a sunhat is definitely advisable. Between May and June and September and October there are pleasantly equable temperatures, and daytime highs are between 16 and 21°C (61 and 70°F). Otherwise, it is unusual to experience climatic extremes or sharp seasonal variations. Average temperatures stay above freezing all year round, and it rarely gets too hot to stay outside in the middle of the day. If you have children you may be tied to school holiday times, but to avoid crowds, try to miss

Everything in the Theme Park is geared to children

popular French holidays, such as Labour Day (Fête du Travail, 1 May), Victory Day (Fête de la Libération, 8 May), Bastille Day (Fête Nationale, 14 July), Assumption (Assomption, 15 August), Hallowe'en/All Saints' (Toussaint, 31 October–1 November), and, of course, Christmas and New Year. You can also expect more crowds around Easter and Whitsuntide. French school holidays are staggered, lasting over several weeks (mid-April to mid-May; early July to early September). August is a traditional holiday month for many Parisians, and those who have not headed for the south coast may well visit the Theme Parks then.

HOW TO BE A LOCAL

Though France is the host country of Disneyland® Resort Paris, both staff ('cast members', as they are known in the resort), and visitors ('guests') are a great mix of nationalities. French and English are the official languages, and you will find notices, show scripts and so on in both. Many of the staff speak one or more other language, particularly German, Dutch, Spanish or Italian. They are young and easy-going, including many students doing a Disney season. Many of the cast members in the Theme Parks and at the hotels are Dutch, chosen for their formidable linguistic skills and their calm, unflappable temperaments. You will obviously find many French staff, too. Their communication skills are impressive, but not always completely fluent. It is always appreciated if you are prepared to meet your hosts halfway, if you have a little French, why not practise it here in this helpful and friendly environment? After all, you will probably need to use it if you have any plans to visit Paris or tour the region afterwards. Apart from language, the mood is American, and the rigorous Disney discipline is imposed, as in US Disney Parks. Everyone is neat and tidy, everyone smiles, and everyone wishes you a nice day. Many of the European cast and guests are still getting used to the Disney approach. Remember to smile a lot. And have a nice day!

CHILDREN

Children of all ages visit Disneyland® Resort Paris; anyone aged 12 or over counts as an adult and must pay the full entrance price. Children under three can enter free. Pricing policies put quite a lot of pressure on families to make

Souvenirs are all part of the fun

the most of every minute they have in the Theme Parks. Unfortunately, children are not always easily programmable. They have a disconcerting habit of not being in the mood for theme-parking on the days you have tickets. Build in some time off, such as a break in the middle of the day, or even a sleep at the hotel. The main thing is to prevent them from becoming overtired. And if the weather is hot, make sure they get enough to drink and are protected from the sun.

The parades and shows, and appearances by Disney

characters in costume, are things most children seem to love. Make sure you have some film in your camera when Mickey Mouse turns up, or you will never be forgiven. You can find **Disney characters** in Disneyland® Park every day, or at 'Character Breakfasts' at Disneyland® Hotel, Disney's New York Hotel® and Café Mickey. For *real* animals, head for **Critter Corral** in **Frontierland**, or visit **Disney's Davy Crockett Ranch**®, where there are ponies to ride in the spring and summer seasons. Electronic **games rooms** and **arcades** in all of the hotels are expensive, but ever-popular with today's hi-tech child.

No two children react in quite the same way to Disneyland® Resort Paris Theme Parks' attractions. Most take them in a matter-of-fact way, and some are completely blasé. Others get wildly excited, a few frightened or sick. It is quite difficult to assess what may alarm a child. Very young ones may find the spooks in **Phantom Manor**, the eerier sections of **Pirates of the Caribbean**, or the Wicked Queen in **Blanche-Neige et les Sept Nains** (Snow White and the Seven Dwarfs) quite perturbing. For further information on attractions for young or older children, and for contra-indications, see **Planning Your Visit** on pages 28–32.)

Facilities

Child facilities are well publicised throughout the

Theme Parks. There is a **Baby Care Center** in Main Street U.S.A. (Disneyland® Park) or behind Studio Services (Walt Disney Studios® Park) where nappies can be changed, bottles warmed and basic necessities purchased. Pushchairs (strollers) can be rented for use within the Theme Parks in **Town Square** (Disneyland® Park) or near Studio Services (Walt Disney Studios® Park). There are no restrictions on pushchairs being brought into the Theme Parks. Lost children will be taken to the **Lost Children Office** and looked after until you find them. And if after enjoying a day with the family in the Theme Parks, parents want to have a night out on their own, Disneyland® Resort Paris is certainly the place to stay since all of the Disneyland® Resort Paris hotels provide baby-sitting services.

Fantasyland's Mad Hatter's Tea Cups ride

TIGHT BUDGET

Taking a family to Disneyland® Resort Paris is by no means a budget holiday option. But there are ways to cut some of the costs, and if you maximise the use of your time at the Theme Parks, it is unlikely that you will feel you have had a poor deal. There is, after all, an enormous amount to do, and if you compare the attractions of Disneyland® Resort Paris Theme Parks with other forms of family entertainment (other Theme Parks, for example, or some museums in central Paris) the inclusive entrance charges begin to look pretty reasonable for such a lot of fun (over 15 hours a day in high season, if you have the stamina).

- Extras can mount up if you are not careful – all the ice creams and soft drinks, the T-shirts and mouse ears. A few of these are part of the experience, but with children in tow you may have to restrain some impulse buys.
- If you have children, or do not mind sharing a bedroom with friends, you can save money by staying in just one room at **Disney's Hotels Cheyenne**® or **Santa Fe**®, or at **Disney's Davy Crockett Ranch**®. Most Disneyland® Resort Paris hotel bedrooms can accommodate families of four; trailer cabins take up to six people. If there are just two of you, it will be

Children are encouraged to participate in the parades

cheaper to stay in a local motel or small hotel near, but not actually in, the resort. But bear transport in mind – you may need a car. If you are relying on public transport, choose an inexpensive hotel somewhere near a convenient metro or RER station in central Paris (preferably on or with easy connections to line A4, the Marne-la-Vallée–Chessy line).

- Choose counter-service cafés or *chariots gourmands* for snacks, rather than more expensive table-service restaurants. If you are feeling very economical, you do not have to buy any food at all. You can bring your own, and eat it in the picnic area *outside* the Theme Parks. You cannot bring any food or drink through the turnstiles. Leave your hamper either in your car, or with Guest Storage near the entrance to Disneyland® Park.
- Try to assess realistically how many days you want to spend at the resort. There is enough at the Theme Parks to keep most people happy for two days, three if you want to revisit some of the attractions. You can save money by buying a three-day passport Theme Park Entrance Ticket, which reduces the adult daily entrance charge by about 25 per cent). You do not have to use it on consecutive days.
- Take some light raingear with you. You will avoid having to spend money on a Mickey Mouse poncho, if it rains.
- Before buying a rail ticket to visit Paris, check what sort of ticket would be best for you – you may be better off buying an inclusive day pass, which allows you as much travel as you like within a 24-hour period, at little more than the normal return rail fare to central Paris. Also have a word with the tourist office outside Marne-la-Vallée Station about museum passes, free maps and so on.
- Take supplies with you of any films, medicines and so on that you may need. Disney hotels, while very comfortable, do not provide quantities of free bath-gel and so forth. What you get is soap and shampoo.
- Above all, keep your children away from video games arcades. All the machines eat €2 pieces at a fearsome rate.

SPORT

Plenty of additional leisure facilities have been built at Disneyland® Resort Paris to cater for the hours of relaxation when guests are not theme-parking and thrill-riding. These facilities are available *only* to guests staying on-site (that is, in appropriate Disney accommodation). If you like an active holiday, the best place to stay within the resort is at **Disney's Davy Crockett Ranch®**. If you are staying at the campsite you can play tennis, volleyball, basketball, football, *pétanque*, ride ponies (if you are small enough), bicycles (if you are not), jog round the running track, or swim in one of the resort's loveliest pools. If you prefer to be a spectator, try out the **Sports Bar** in **Disney® Village**, where numerous TV sets show an endless round of sports programmes. Non-stop sports channels are available on Disneyland® Resort Paris's hotel television network, too. All the hotels, and Disney® Village, have games rooms with a variety of video simulator games and other activities. Children's playgrounds are available at several of the hotels, and at the campsite. The stockaded Fort Apache and Indian wigwams are fun at **Disney's Hotel Cheyenne®**.

Boating

The excitingly landscaped water-courses of Frontierland, the **Rivers of the Far West**, which run around that interesting piece of Arizona called **Big Thunder Mountain**, provide Disneyland® Resort Paris guests with an opportunity to take a break from the excitement of the Theme Parks' attractions and to cool down on a hot, sunny day. They can traverse these waters in various craft: **River Rogue Keelboats**, or two Mississippi-style **Paddlewheel Riverboats**. These rides, of course, are free once you are inside Disneyland® Park, but they are popular and you may have a long wait for them on days when the Theme Park is crowded. (Refer also to **What to See** on pages 46 and 48.)

Fun in Fantasyland

Cycle Hire

At **Disney's Davy Crockett Ranch®** bicycles are available for hire by guests staying at the campsite only.

Golf

The campsite is conveniently close to the golf course, and it is open to the public. Golf Disneyland® Paris is a championship course designed to host top tournaments, but less ambitious golfers of all abilities are welcome to test their skills. Lakes, hills, waterfalls, rocks and the most Disneyish bunkers have been magically bulldozed from flat arable fields, creating a series of varied landscapes which will eventually be sheltered by lush vegetation. Each of the three nine-hole sections of the course is rated Par 36, with lengths ranging from 6,781 yards (6,221m) for the championship course to 5,513 yards (5,058m) for the junior course. All facilities are provided: electric golf carts, a driving range, golf-bag storage and a putting green (in the shape of Mickey Mouse's head). The 19th hole has been provided, of course, at the circular **Clubhouse Grill**, whose windows overlook the putting green. Inside are showers, lockers, a bar and restaurant, and television room. Coaching, a repair and hire service, and a shop selling golfing equipment are also on-site. You can test all aspects of your game in the training area. Group and package rates, and less expensive 'twilight' green fees, are also available. The course is open every day from 8am (or 9am, depending on the season) till sunset.

Health Clubs

The four more up-market hotels (**Disneyland® Hotel**, **Disney's Hotel New York®**, **Disney's Newport Bay Club®** and **Disney's Sequoia Lodge®**) have health clubs with gyms, saunas, solariums, massage, steam rooms, jacuzzis, and so on. They are free to hotel guests, but a charge is payable for the solarium and massage.

Ice-skating

That colourful ornamental pond outside **Disney's Hotel New York®** freezes over during the winter months and members of the public can use it during three daily sesssions. It costs €9.15 per session (€7.62 if you bring your own skates); €6.10 and €4.57 respectively for under-12s.

Jogging

There are two jogging trails, one around **Lake Disney®**, and one winding through the forest in **Disney's Davy Crockett Ranch®**. They are for use by resort hotel and campsite guests only.

Swimming Pools

If you are staying in Disney accommodation, one thing you should definitely bring is swim-wear. The four most expensive hotels, plus **Disney's Davy Crockett Ranch®**, have heated pools. They are large and imaginatively designed, perhaps the most interesting being the one at the wildness retreat and the pool at **Disney's**

Ice-skating is popular in winter

Sequoia Lodge®, with its rocky waterfalls and woodland scenery. Disneyland® Resort Paris guests should only use the facilities available where they are staying.

Tennis

There are four hard outdoor courts at Disneyland® Resort Paris: two at **Disney's Davy Crockett Ranch®** and two at **Disney's Hotel New York®** (the ones at Hotel New York® are floodlit at night and may be used by other Disney hotel guests). There is a charge for use of the courts and reservations must be made. Racquets and balls can be hired on site, but do remember to pack suitable clothes and shoes.

Other Options

If you are staying off-site (i.e. not in Disney accommodation), or fancy a whole day of sports activities, you can visit an outdoor leisure centre at **Jablines**, which can be reached from the N3 (exit at Claye Souilly). Visitors have access to lake swimming (sand beach), riding, tennis, archery, mini-golf, sailing, windsurfing and so on. A single modest entrance charge admits you to the centre; activities are extra. Groups can stay overnight; there is also a campsite. For information about Jablines, ask at the tourist office outside Marne-la-Vallée Station.

Directory

This section (with the biscuit-coloured band) contains day-to-day information, including travel, money matters and reservations.

Contents

Arriving

By Air

Most international scheduled flights, including British Airways, Air France, Aer Lingus, SAS and Finnair, land at Roissy–Charles de Gaulle airport, about 15 miles (24km) northeast of Paris (tel: 01 48 62 22 80). The other option is Orly, just over 10 miles (17km) south of Paris (tel: 01 49 75 15 15). Both airports are served by shuttle buses (*navettes*) which depart for Disneyland® Resort Paris every 20 minutes at peak times, every hour at other times. Journey times vary according to traffic density. Buses cost the same from either airport (adult €12.96, child €9.91; transfer fares are included in Disney hotel packages). Passengers are taken to each of the Disneyland® Resort Paris hotels in turn, or dropped at the bus station, very near the entrance of the Theme Parks. If you are staying at Disney's Davy Crockett Ranch®, you will have to get a taxi from the station to the campsite.

The Queen of Hearts' Castle

By Rail

The Parisian suburban railway (RER) now extends as far as Disneyland® Resort Paris. The station is Marne-la-Vallée–Chessy, about two minutes' walk from the entrances of both Theme Parks. Journey time is about 40 minutes from central Paris (Châtelet–les–Halles Métro link), but you need to be careful which train you take. It is a branched line (take Line A4, not Line A2 for Boissy–St-Léger), and not all the trains continue as far as Marne-la-Vallée. Check the platform indicators before you board, and make sure the correct light is showing. The single fare is €5.95 (2002 price). Trains run until about midnight. The high-speed TGV train now stops at Marne-la-Vallée–Chessy Station, putting Disneyland® Resort Paris just 1 hour 48 minutes from Lyon, 63 minutes from Lille and only 3 hours from London's Waterloo Station via the Euro Tunnel.

By Car
Disneyland® Resort Paris lies about 20 miles (32km) due east of Paris, off exit 14 of the A4 Nancy–Metz motorway (the route to Strasbourg) in the sprawling area of Marne-la-Vallée, *département* Seine-et-Marne. If you approach from another direction, to avoid the capital, you will probably use the Francilienne (A104 and N104), linking motorways A1 (*Autoroute du Nord*, bound for the Channel ports, UK and Low Countries), A4 (*Autoroute de l'Est*, leading to Germany, Austria and Luxembourg), A6 (*Autoroute du Soleil*, heading south for the Riviera, Italy and Switzerland), and A10 (*L'Aquitaine*, which goes via Bordeaux towards Spain and Portugal). Follow signs to Marne-la-Vallée (Val d'Europe) until you see signposts for the resort. French motorways are toll roads, but they are free in the Paris area.
Leave the motorway at exit 14 and follow signs for the Theme Parks. If you are staying at a Disney hotel you can use the hotel car park; if not, park in the main lot (€7 per day – 2002 prices). The car park is huge (space for over 9,000 vehicles), so note carefully where you leave your car. Each sector is named after a Disney character. Moving walkways speed up the journey from the car park to the main entrances. Cars cannot be left overnight in the car park. If you have engine trouble, or forget where you left your car, ask cast members for help.

Marne-la-Vallée–Chessy Station is right on the Theme Parks' doorstep

Cameras, Films and Photography
Films, batteries and a developing service are available in any hotel shop and

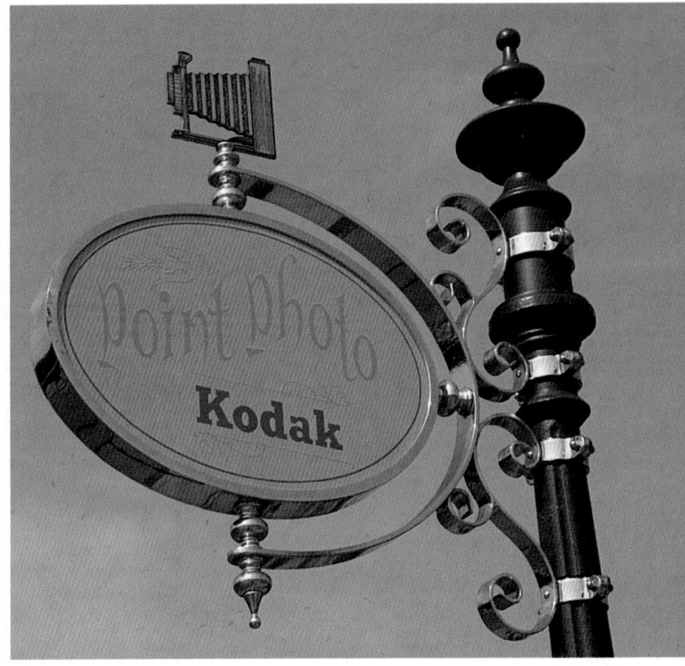

'Point Photo' signs appear throughout Disneyland® Park

at several shops in the Theme Parks. The specialist photographic equipment store is **Town Square Photography** in Main Street, U.S.A., where you can buy or rent cameras and video cameras, and have film developed the same day. **Studio Photo** in Walt Disney Studios® Park (Front Lot) sells cameras and film, and **Walt Disney Studios Store** offers a photo development service. Look for the 'Point Photo' signs, which show good places for a picture. You are not allowed to take flash photographs, or to use video cameras within attractions.

Car Hire
Hertz is the official Disneyland® Resort Paris car-hire company, with a rental office in Marne-la-Vallée-Chessy TGV/RER Station. Guests staying at the resort receive concessionary rates, which are pretty competitive. If you are based at the resort and just want a car to tour the area for a few days, this is by far the most convenient way to do it. Take the minibus from the hotel to the rental office. If you are staying off-site, check out competing rates at various airport offices. You can also book cars through Disneyland® Resort Paris's **Central Reservations Office** (see page 121).

First Aid and Medical
First-aid centres with fully trained nursing staff are located next to **Plaza Gardens Restaurant** in Main Street, U.S.A. and behind **Studio Services** in Front Lot. Simple medical supplies can be found in all the hotels. If there is a serious problem, ask your hotel receptionist or the tourist office for advice. There is a pharmacy in **Coupvray**, a medical centre in **Esbly**, and a hospital in **Lagny**. Foreign visitors are advised to take out adequate medical insurance, even if they are EC residents, either independently or through your travel agent.

Guided Tours
These can be booked from **City Hall** in Town Square and **Studio Services** in Front Lot. They last between 1 and 2 hours. (Special tours for private groups by arrangement.)

Language
The two official languages in the Theme Parks are French and English. Visual clues are

Moving sidewalks help take guests from Guest Parking to the Theme Park entrance gates

used wherever possible, but written signs, where they are needed, may be in either or both languages. You will learn some interesting new vocabulary. The shows requiring dialogue mix and match the two languages (with varying success). Most cast members speak the two official languages (not always fluently), and possibly others, the most usual being German, Spanish or Italian. In Disneyland® Resort Paris accommodation there is always someone who can speak these languages.

Lost People and Lost Property
Stray children are taken to the **Lost Children Office** on Central Plaza or at Studio Services, where they are looked after until their guardians turn up. Enquire for them here, at any information booth, at **Guest Relations**, or at **City Hall**. Lost or found property should be notified to **City Hall** in Town Square or **Studio Services** in Front Lot, where you can also leave a message for separated companions. If you lose anything in your hotel, contact **Housekeeping**. Safe deposit boxes are provided at all reception areas.

Media – Radio, TV, Newspapers
All bedrooms in Disneyland® Resort Paris hotels are equipped with cable television, currently receiving five French channels as well as international channels, including BBC World, CNBC and Eurosport, plus three Disney channels, which relay closed-circuit information and Disney films. There are several radio stations, mostly featuring music. A wide variety of foreign newspapers and magazines is available in hotel shops and at the RER station.

Money Matters
Exchange facilities can be found at the **Main Entrances**, and in the two information booths in **Adventureland** and **Fantasyland**. You can also change money in **Disney® Village**, and at any

accommodation reception desk (if you are a resident). The rates given are standard throughout the resort. They are on the low side, but service is pleasant and efficient, and no commission is charged. You may get a slightly better commission-free rate in central Paris if you happen to be there, but it is not worth making a special journey. Remember that you will need your passport if you want to change traveller's cheques. Cash dispensers are available in the two arcades in **Main Street, U.S.A.**, in **Discoveryland**, **Adventureland**, next to **Studio Services** and at the **Backlot Express Restaurant**.
All shops and hotels, most restaurants and the campsite will accept major credit cards (American Express, Visa, Eurocard/Mastercard); personal or traveller's cheques drawn in euros (with valid ID), Eurocheques or banknotes (euros). Disneyland® Resort Paris hotel guests may charge items to their hotel accounts using a special card which they receive as they check in.

Opening Times
Disneyland® Resort Paris Theme Parks can be visited 365 days a year. Officially, the Theme Parks open at 9am most days (10am from September to mid-March), but often it is open earlier. Disneyland® Resort Paris guests will find little notes in their bedrooms saying 'Just for you, the Theme Parks open earlier'. Actually, anyone who turns up can get in. During peak seasons, you can usually get inside the gates at least half an hour before the official opening time, though attractions open at the usual time. Weekdays are generally less busy than weekends, and Tuesday is an especially quiet day. On Mondays many shops and other businesses are closed and families often go out together. Schools have the day off on Wednesdays, so this is a popular day with French children. Closing times change according to season, holiday periods, weather conditions and demand. Although the turnstiles may allow no more visitors in if the Theme Parks become too crowded, guests staying in Disneyland® Resort Paris accommodation always have entry. Check what time the Theme Parks close as you enter: in high summer Disneyland® Park often stays open until 11pm. (For full details tel: 08705 03 03 03.)
Some of the shops and restaurants in Disney® Village stay open all day; others open in the evening and keep going until well after midnight. Hurricanes nightclub shuts at 5am at the latest, but most other night spots close at 1am. The post office stays open until 7pm, but exact times vary according to season.
Most hotel restaurants serve dinner until 11pm; bars may stay open later (but not all bars open at lunchtime). The best hotel venue for an all-day light snack is the Parkside Diner in Disney's Hotel New York®.
The golf course is open from 8am or 9am until sunset, and the Clubhouse Grill stays open until one hour after sunset.

Pets
The only animals allowed within the resort to compete with Mickey and friends are guide dogs. Near the car park is the **Animal Care Center**, where trained staff will care for your dog for a charge of €8 per day, including food and exercise (€12 extra overnight – 2002 prices). However, pets are only accepted at the Animal Care Center if owners can produce relevant certificates of health, or proof of vaccination.

Police
Disneyland® Resort Paris makes its own security arrangements, very discreetly but very efficiently. Security staff can be summoned instantly to any trouble spot. Outside the Theme Parks, phone 17 if there has been an accident or you need the police; phone 18 for the fire brigade. Take sensible precautions with your belongings, as in any crowded place. Remember to lock your car, and to leave belongings where they are out of sight.

Post Office
This can be found at Marne-la-Vallée Station and is usually open from 9am till 7pm, seven days a week, but not on public holidays. Stamps can be bought at many shops, including **The Storybook Store** in Town Square, inside Disneyland® Park. Postboxes can be found throughout the Theme Parks, and in the hotels and Disney's Davy Crockett Ranch®.

Fairytale characters add to the fun

The walkway to Space Mountain – before the crowds arrive

Reservations
To reserve accommodation or to hire cars at Disneyland® Resort Paris, just call Reservations on 08705 03 03 03 (national rate call), seven days a week. From Ireland, dial 00 44 8705 03 03 03 (international rate call) from Monday to Friday 8am– 8pm, Saturday 9am– 6pm (5pm on Sunday). You can also visit the Disneyland® Resort Paris website: http://www.disneylandparis.co.uk or www.disneylandparis.com for information only. From France call 01 60 30 60 30.

Senior Citizens
Groups of 25 senior citizens (over 55s) or more qualify for a 20 per cent reduction in Theme Park entrance fees (this offer may not be valid during peak periods). Cast members are always happy to help anyone with special needs. It may be worth getting a *Carte*

Senior, which is valid for all women over 60 and all men over 65, and entitles the bearer to reductions of up to 50 per cent in Paris museums, on public transport and in places of entertainment. The card costs €45 for unlimited travel (2002 price). To get one, simply take your passport to the *Abonnement* office of any main railway station. The card is valid for a year. If you do not have one, wave your passport when you have to pay and you may still be able to get a discount.

Telephones

Both coin-operated and card phones are available in the Theme Parks, in Disney® Village and in resort accommodation. France Télécom phone cards are on sale at the post office, in shops, and at the golf course. Telephone charges are the same in all hotels and in the campsite. They include a mark-up over normal France Télécom rates, depending upon what time of day you call.

Tipping

As a rule, it is not necessary to leave tips in Disneyland® Resort Paris, however you may feel inclined to leave something in a table-service restaurant, or to tip a member of staff who has been particularly helpful. Outside the Theme Parks check whether service is included (*service compris*) before you pay the bill. It is customary to leave small change in a saucer at a

Signs use pictures where possible

bar or café. Porters, cinema usherettes, tour guides and Paris's cabbies all expect tips.

Toilets
There are lots of these, discreetly placed around the resort. They are regularly cleaned and serviced and mostly exemplary, though some are a little cramped. What you will find outside the resort, however, is another matter – and mostly best forgotten.

Tourist Office
Seine-et-Marne and Île-de-France tourist office is situated outside Marne-la-Vallee Station and is a very good source of information and leaflets on local sights, hotels and restaurants. There is also a video and laser presentation. It is well worth a visit (tel: 01 60 43 33 33). See also **Excursions from Disneyland® Paris Theme Park**, on pages 72–5.

Travellers with Disabilities
Ask for the *Disabled Guest Guide* at the main entrance, City Hall or at Studio Services. This gives full details of facilities for disabled visitors. The resort is designed to be as user-friendly as possible for all guests, but wheelchair users will need someone in their

party who can lift them out of their chair and on to rides. Special vehicles can be provided to help guests reach the Theme Parks from the hotels or campsite, and all hotels have rooms designed for the disabled. Parking spaces near the entrance are also available. Wheelchairs can be rented in **Town Square** in Main Street U.S.A or at **Studio Services** in Front Lot (€6.10 per day; they must not be taken outside the Theme Parks). Priority is given to the disabled for places to see parades and shows. Ask any cast member for advice. All WC blocks, shops and restaurants are accessible by wheelchair, and some shops have special dressing-rooms. If you need assistance, enquire at **City Hall**, **First Aid** (near Plaza Gardens Restaurant) or **Studio Services**.

If you have a weak back or neck, avoid the joltier rides such as **Big Thunder Mountain**, **Indiana Jones™ and the Temple of Peril: Backwards**, **Space Mountain**, **Star Tours** and **Rock'n'Roller Coaster starring Aerosmith**. Special aids are available for sight-impaired guests.

Take time out to enjoy a round of golf at Disneyland® Paris

LANGUAGE

Basic Vocabulary

yes oui
no non
please s'il vous plaît
thank you merci
hello/good morning bonjour
good evening bonsoir
goodbye au revoir
excuse me excusez moi
I am sorry pardon
later plus tard
now maintenant
small petit
today aujourd'hui
yesterday hier
tomorrow demain
week une semaine
when? quand?
why? pourquoi?
with avec
without sans
prohibited interdit
closed fermé
open ouvert
shop le magasin
stamps les timbres
bank/exchange la banque/le bureau de change
money argent
traveller's cheques chèques de voyage

Useful Phrases

do you speak English? parlez-vous anglais?
at what time? à quelle heure?
I do not understand je ne comprends pas
I would like je voudrais
this one ceci
that one cela
how much is it? c'est combien?

Directions and Getting Around

here ici
there là

near près
before avant
in front of devant
behind derrière
opposite en face de
right à droite
left à gauche
straight on tout droit
street la rue
car parking le parking
petrol l'essence
underground station la station du métro
railway station la gare
ticket office le guichet
ticket le billet
ten metro tickets un carnet
a single ticket un aller simple
please direct me to pour aller à… s'il vous plaît
the road for la route de
traffic lights les feux
my car has broken down ma voiture est en panne

Numbers

one un (e)

Shopping for souvenirs is part of the entertainment at Disneyland Paris

two deux
three trois
four quatre
five cinq
six six
seven sept
eight huit
nine neuf
ten dix
first premier (-ière)
second deuxième, second (e)

Days of the Week
Monday lundi
Tuesday mardi
Wednesday mercredi
Thursday jeudi
Friday vendredi
Saturday samedi
Sunday dimanche

Months of the Year
January janvier
February février
March mars
April avril
May mai
June juin
July juillet
August août
September septembre
October octobre
November novembre
December décembre
Christmas Noël
Easter Pâques
festivals/holidays fêtes/jours fériés

Eating and Drinking
to eat manger
to drink boire
coffee le café
tea le thé
black/white noir/au lait
fresh orange juice une orange pressée
hot chocolate chocolat chaud
milk lait
mineral water l'eau minérale
a beer une bière
wine – white/red le vin – blanc/rouge
wine list la carte des vins
cheapest fixed-price menu menu conseillé
fixed-price menu prix fixe
self service libre service (le self)
waitress/waiter mademoiselle/monsieur
where are the toilets? où sont les toilettes?
all included service compris
menu la carte
first course hors d'œuvre/entrée
second course (main course) plat principal
cheese fromage
dessert les desserts
snack casse-croûte, snack
may I have the bill? l'addition, s'il vous plaît?

INDEX

Page numbers in *italics* refer to illustrations

INDEX

ACKNOWLEDGEMENTS

The Automobile Association also wishes to thank the following photographers and libraries for their assistance in the preparation of this book:
ANTONY SOUTER was commissioned by the **AA Photo Library** to take all the photographs for this book except those listed below:
AA PHOTO LIBRARY 74/5 Fontainebleau Palace (**David Noble**)
© **THE WALT DISNEY COMPANY** F/cover (c) girl, bottom Walt Disney Studios, 4, 8/9, 11, 15, 16/17, 20, 22/3, 27, 28/9, 31, 32, 33, 35, 36/7, 38/9, 40, 41, 44, 49, 50/1, 52, 53, 60, 61, 66, 68/9, 70, 71, 88/9, 90, 93, 97, 98, 100, 108, 109, 111, 119, 120/1, 122/3

Contributors
For original edition: Copy editors Ron Hawkins and Edwina Johnson
For this revision: Researcher/verifier Elisabeth Morris
Thanks also to **Disneyland® Resort Paris** for their assistance.